Bathroom Design

Badezimmer Design

Design de salle de bains

Baños de diseño

teNeues

Editor in chief: Paco Asensio

Texts: Marina Ubach

Editorial coordination: Cynthia Reschke

Editorial assistant: Simone K. Schleifer

Art director: Mireia Casanovas Soley

Layout: Ignasi Gràcia Blanco

Copy-editing: Francesc Bombí-Vilaseca

German translation: Sven Mettner, Oliver Herzig

French translation: Catherine Reschke

English translation: Books Factory *Translations*

Published by teNeues Publishing Group

teNeues Publishing Company
16 West 22nd Street, New York, NY 10010, US
Tel.: 001-212-627-9090, Fax: 001-212-627-9511

teNeues Book Division
Kaistraße 18
40221 Düsseldorf, Germany
Tel.: 0049-(0)211-994597-0, Fax: 0049-(0)211-994597-40

teNeues Publishing UK Ltd.
P.O. Box 402
West Byfleet
KT14 7ZF, Great Britain
Tel.: 0044-1932-403509, Fax: 0044-1932-403514

www.teneues.com

ISBN: 3-8238-4523-3

Editorial project: © 2003 **LOFT** Publications

Via Laietana, 32 4° Of. 92
08003 Barcelona, Spain
Tel.: 0034 932 688 088
Fax: 0034 932 687 073

e-mail: loft@loftpublications.com
www.loftpublications.com

Printed by: Gràfiques Anman del Vallès. Barberà del Vallès. Spain 2003

Bibliographic information published by Die Deutsche Bibliothek
Die Deutsche Bibliothek lists this publication in the Deutsche
Nationalbibliographie; detailed bibliographic data is available in
the Internet at http://dnb.ddb.de.

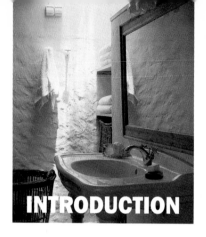

INTRODUCTION

EINLEITUNG

Throughout the course of history, baths have undergone a complete transformation, evolving with the passage of time and the customs and characteristics of each period and culture. In antiquity, bathing was already synonymous with ritual. The bath was a space for the practice of body cult and even, in the case of public baths, for meeting. In other times, hygiene was not a priority among the social classes. Consequently, the bathroom was practically non-existent or, at least, it did not have a fixed place in the home. During several decades, toilets and bathtubs shifted from room to room, according to their use. In the 19th-century, preoccupation with hygiene increased. Bathrooms began to occupy their own space and be considered as environments independent from the rest of the house. New technologies introduced new models, materials and coverings more resistant to humidity and water. These were selected, in terms of decoration, according to the tastes and personality of the owner. Gradually, bathrooms acquired prominence as the sole place for hygiene and prolongation of rest. Today, they are

Im Laufe der Geschichte haben Bäder einen grundlegenden Wandel erfahren und sich in Abhängigkeit der Gewohnheiten und Charakteristika der jeweiligen Epoche oder Kultur stetig weiterentwickelt. In der Antike war „ein Bad nehmen" gleichbedeutend mit einem Ritual. Das Badezimmer war ein Ort für den Körperkult und in öffentlichen Bädern sogar für Versammlungen. In anderen Epochen hingegen, wurde der Hygiene in keiner der sozialen Schichten eine große Bedeutung beigemessen, und das Badezimmer war praktisch nicht vorhanden oder nahm zumindest keinen festen Platz in der Wohnung ein. In einigen Jahrzehnten wurden Toilette und Bad auch je nach Notwendigkeit zwischen den Zimmern verschoben. Im 19. Jahrhundert gewann die Hygiene einen größeren Stellenwert. Man gab dem Bad einen eigenen Platz in der Wohnung, den man unabhängig vom restlichen Haus als einen selbständigen Raum betrachtete. Die Weiterentwicklung der Technologie führte zu neuen Modellen, Materialien und Verkleidungen, die widerstandsfähiger gegen Feuchtigkeit und Wasser waren

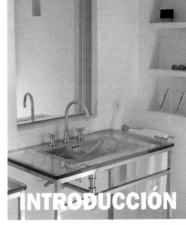

INTRODUCTION

INTRODUCCIÓN

Les salles de bains ont subit une transformation complète au cours de l'histoire, évoluant au fil des années, des coutumes et des caractéristiques propres à chaque époque et chaque culture. Dans l'antiquité, prendre un bain était synonyme de rituel, représentant un culte du corps et également, dans les bains publiques, un lieu de rencontre. A d'autres époques, l'hygiène n'est même pas particulière à certaines classes sociales, les salles de bains étant pratiquement inexistantes ou n'ayant pas de place définie à l'intérieur des habitations. Durant plusieurs décades, on déplace les toilettes et les baignoires d'une chambre à l'autre en fonction de leur usage. Au XIXème siècle on se préoccupe plus de l'hygiène. On octroie aux salles de bains une place propre et on les considère comme une pièce indépendante au sein de la maison. Les technologies nouvelles amenèrent de nouveaux modèles, ainsi que des matériaux et revêtements plus résistant à l'humidité et à l'eau. On les choisit en tenant compte de leur aspect décoratif et en les adaptant au goût et à la personnalité des propriétaires. Peu à

Los baños han sufrido una completa transformación a lo largo de la historia, evolucionando con el paso de los años, las costumbres y las características de cada época y cultura. Ya en la antigüedad, tomar un baño era sinónimo de ritual, espacio de culto al cuerpo e incluso, en los baños públicos, lugar de reunión. En otras épocas, la higiene no era precisamente una prioridad entre las clases sociales, por lo que el baño era prácticamente inexistente o bien no tenía un lugar fijo en la vivienda. Durante algunas décadas, los sanitarios y la bañera fueron trasladándose de habitación en habitación, en función de su uso. En el siglo XIX la preocupación por la higiene aumentó y los baños empiezaron a ubicarse en un espacio propio, considerado un ambiente independiente del resto de la casa. Las nuevas tecnologías introducen nuevos modelos, materiales y revestimientos más resistentes a la humedad y al agua. Se eligen con intención decorativa, en función del gusto y la personalidad del propietario. Poco a poco, los cuartos de baño van adquiriendo protagonismo como único espacio para la hi-

designed to be spacious rooms with light, with demarcated areas, or, in the case of small bathrooms, with practical solutions in order to take maximum advantage of space. The objective is granting the bathroom a functional use while at the same time making it an area for rest and relaxation. All of this is sought without having to sacrifice the intimacy which, it goes without saying, this special room requires. New designs advocate the combination of traditional materials (wood, glass, ceramic and marble) with highly resistant, easy-to-maintain, innovative coverings (porcelains, resins). New technological advances in all types of toilets and general installations are not neglected. An example is the use of home automation, the first step in the configuration of the bathroom of the future. There exist many designs for a classical or an avant-garde bathroom, for one of rustic-

und sich in ihrer dekorativen Wirkung nach dem Geschmack und der Persönlichkeit des Besitzers richteten. Nach und nach gewannen Bäder den Statuts des alleinigen Raumes für Hygiene. Heutzutage werden sie als ausgedehnte Räume mit Licht und klar abgegrenzten Zonen, oder aber im Falle von kleinen Bädern, als Räume mit praktischen Lösungen zur optimalen Platzausnutzung entworfen, mit dem Ziel, dem Benutzer einen funktionellen Gebrauch zu garantieren und zugleich als Relax- und Ruhezone zu dienen. All dies wird ohne Verzicht auf Intimität erreicht, welche dieser Raum zweifelsohne in einer ganz speziellen Weise bewahren sollte. Beim Design werden traditionelle Materialien wie Holz, Glas, Keramik und Marmor mit innovativen, sehr widerstandsfähigen und leicht zu pflegenden Beschichtungen wie Porzellane und Harze kombiniert. Auch die

peu, les salles de bains acquièrent un rôle principal d'espace unique destiné à l'hygiène et à la détente. De nos jours elles sont conçues comme des pièces spacieuses et lumineuses dans un espace délimité mais aussi comme de petites pièces proposant des solutions très pratiques pour en tirer le meilleur parti. Elles sont d'une grande fonctionnalité permettant pourtant de se détendre et se reposer. Tout cela, sans avoir à renoncer à l'intimité nécessaire à ce lieu. Le nouveau design plaide en faveur des matériaux classiques (le bois, le verre, la céramique et le marbre) avec des revêtements innovateurs de grande résistance et faciles à entretenir (porcelaines, résines…), sans pourtant négliger les progrès techniques des toilettes et des diverses installations. L'automatisation représentant le premier pas dans la conception des salles de bains du future.

giene y prolongación del descanso. En la actua-lidad, se proyectan amplias habitaciones con luz, con zonas bien delimitadas, o bien pequeños baños con soluciones muy prácticas para aprovechar al máximo el espacio, con la intención de que los usuarios puedan dar al baño un uso funcional y destinarlo, a la vez, a zona de relax y descanso. Y todo ello sin tener que renunciar a la intimidad que, sin duda, necesita esta estancia de forma especial. Los nuevos diseños abogan por la combinación de materiales tradicionales (la madera, el cristal, la cerá-mica y el mármol) con revestimientos innovadores de gran resistencia y fácil mantenimiento (porcelanas, resinas…), sin descuidar los nuevos avances tecnológicos en todo tipo de sanitarios e instalaciones generales, como la aplicación de la domótica, que constituye el primer paso para configurar el baño del futuro. En la

style or stylized minimalist form, designs with an eye to the past or those directed towards more modern styles. Scandinavian and Japanese influences have resulted in a change of attitude toward the bathroom. Bathrooms have come to be regarded as natural spaces in which health and relaxation are complementary. New accessories and details add personality to the room and permit a considerable increase in functionality. Today´s bathroom has adapted to the strongest demands in its transformation into a small paradise of peace and intimacy.

stetige technische Weiterentwicklung der Toiletten und anderer sanitärer Installationen ist nicht zu vernachlässigen, und hierfür stellt die Automatisierung einen ersten Schritt in Richtung zukünftiger Bäder dar. Gegenwärtig gibt es vielfältige Gestaltungsmöglichkeiten, die es erlauben, das Bad im klassischen oder fortschrittlichen Stil, rustikal oder mit ausgesucht minimalistischen Formen, mit Blick in die Vergangenheit oder im Einklang mit den modernsten Stilrichtungen einzurichten. Skandinavische und japanische Einflüsse haben zu einer veränderten Haltung gegenüber dem Bad geführt, das dort als ein „natürlicher Raum" angesehen wird, in dem Gesundheit und Ruhe gleichbedeutend sind. Neuartige Accessoires und Details geben dem Raum eine persönliche Note und machen seine Benutzung spürbar funktionaler. Das Badezimmer von Heute hat sich durch seinen Wandel zu einem kleinen Paradies des Friedens und der Intimität entwickelt und sich an die gewachsenen Anforderungen seiner Benutzer angepasst.

Il existe d'innombrables designs allant d'une conception de salle de bains classique ou avant-gardiste, ayant un style rustique ou des formes stylisées et minimalistes, jettent un clin d'œil au passé ou encore celle dirigée vers les styles les plus modernes. Les influences scandinaves et japonaises ont provoqué un changement d'attitude face à la salle de bains en faisant un espace naturel dans lequel la santé et la relaxation se complètent. Des nouveaux accessoires et détails y ajoutent de la personnalité et permettent d'en augmenter la fonctionnalité. De nos jours la salle de bains s'est adaptée aux exigences les plus grandes se transformant ainsi en un petit paradis paisible et intime.

actualidad existen múltiples propuestas que permiten proyectar un baño clásico o muy vanguardista, de estilo rústico o de estilizadas formas minimalistas, con una mirada al pasado o en consonancia con los estilos más modernos. Las influencias escandinavas y japonesas han permitido un razonable cambio de actitud en el baño que conforman un espacio natural en el que la salud y la relajación se complementan. Los nuevos accesorios y detalles añaden personalidad a la estancia y permiten que su uso sea mucho más funcional. El baño actual se ha adaptado a las máximas exigencias para convertirse en un pequeño paraíso de paz e intimidad.

HISTORY
AND

L'histoire de l'hygiène et de la salle de bains

Die Geschichte der Hygiene und des Badezimmers

OF HYGIENE BATHS

Historia de la higiene y el baño

Evolution of baths

To speak with any authority about the history of baths, we must first look to ancient civilizations that carried out purification ceremonies and ancestral rites with water. These practices should not be confused as having a hygienic function, but rather viewed as purely religious in nature. Water was considered wholesome for the body, symbolic of purity and the immortality of the soul. In many cultures (e.g., Egyptian Jewish, Mesopotamian and Hindu), cleansing of the body was required as a symbolic act of purification prior to entering sacred places. Thus, the ritual baths of the Hindus in the Ganges and the ablutions practised by the ancient Egyptians in the Nile in order to purify themselves and to pay tribute to the dead, are well documented.

In the majority of ancient civilizations (Indian, Egyptian, Chinese, Mesopotamian, Greco-Roman, Islamic and pre-Columbian), homes corresponded to the house-patio structure. Each was arranged as a small autonomous village, with areas reserved for liturgical ceremonies.

Die Entwicklung des Badezimmers

Um die Geschichte des Bades zu veranschaulichen, ist es notwendig zu den alten Zivilisationen zurückzukehren, und die überlieferten Rituale und Reinigungszeremonien mit Wasser zu betrachten. Diese Handlungen dienten nicht der Hygiene, sondern hatten ausschließlich religiösen Charakter. Wasser wurde als Heilmittel für den Körper und sogar als Symbol der Reinheit und Unsterblichkeit der Seele angesehen. In vielen Kulturen (wie der ägyptischen, jüdischen, mesopotamischen oder hinduistischen) setzte sich die Reinigung des Körpers als ein Sinnbild der Läuterung durch, die vor Betreten einer heiligen Stätte vollzogen werden musste. So diente beispielsweise das Bad der Hindus im Ganges der Befreiung von bösen Geistern, das der alten Ägypter im Nil war neben der Reinwaschung auch ein Tribut an die Verstorbenen.

In der Mehrzahl dieser alten Kulturen wurde eine Art von Wohnhaus errichtet, die einer Haus-und-Hof-Struktur entsprach. Jedes Wohnhaus war wie ein kleines unabhängiges Dorf aufgebaut,

L'évolution de la salle de bain

Pour parler de l'histoire des bains, nous devons retourner aux civilisations antiques, qui pratiquaient des cérémonies de purification et des rites ancestraux avec l'eau. Cela n'avait rien à voir avec l'hygiène et avait un sens purement religieux. L'eau était considérée comme un remède pour le corps, un symbole de pureté et de l'immortalité de l'âme. Dans beaucoup de cultures (comme les cultures égyptienne, juive, mésopotamienne ou hindoue) la propreté corporelle s'imposa comme symbole de purification avant de pénétrer dans des lieux sacrés. Les hindous, par exemple, se baignaient dans le Gange pour se débarasser des mauvais esprits de même que chez les Egyptiens les ablutions dans le Nil étaient, en dehors d'une purification, un hommage aux défunts.

Dans la plupart des cultures antiques, on contruisait une sorte de demeure qui avait la structure d'une maison-patio. Chaque habitation était bâtie comme un tout petit village autonome avec des parties destinées aux cérémonies liturgiques.

Evolución del baño

Para hablar de la historia del baño hemos de remitirnos a las antiguas civilizaciones, que practicaban ceremonias purificadoras y ritos ancestrales con agua, por lo que estas prácticas no deben confundirse con una función higiénica, sino puramente religiosa. El agua era considerada sanadora del cuerpo, símbolo de pureza e incluso de la inmortalidad del alma. En muchas culturas (como la egipcia, la judía, la mesopotámica o la hindú) se imponía la práctica de la limpieza corporal como símbolo de purificación, antes de entrar en lugares sagrados. En este sentido, son conocidos los baños rituales que los hindúes practican en el Ganges, y las abluciones a que los antiguos egipcios se sometían en el Nilo con la intención de purificarse y rendir tributo a los difuntos.

El tipo de vivienda que se estableció en la mayoría de dichas culturas de la antigüedad correspondía a la estructura de casa-patio. Cada vivienda se estructuraba como un pequeño poblado autónomo, con parcelas destinadas a las ceremonias litúrgicas.

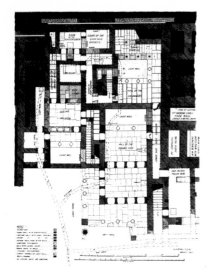

The earliest indications of baths date back to the third millennium B.C. and can be divided into two categories: steam baths (mainly in Europe, America and Asia) and cold baths (Asia), the latter erected in ephemeral structures or permanent areas. Communal baths were set up separately from the village quarters and used as means of keeping away evil spirits or paying tribute to the deceased.

The oldest bathtub dates back to the year 1700 B.C. and pertained to the palace of Knossos in Crete. Its similarity to present-day bathtubs is startling, as also is its system of sanitary plumbing.

Greek civilization incorporated bathing into various mythological accounts. Homer, for example, describes mythological warriors bathing in warm water in order to regain strength and continue the fight. The Olympian Gods also claimed

mit Bereichen, welche für liturgische Zeremonien bestimmt war.

Die frühesten Indizien für Bäder in Wohnhäusern sind in das dritte Jahrtausend vor Christus datiert und können in zwei Typen unterschieden werden: Dampfbäder (vorwiegend in Europa, Amerika und Asien) und Kaltbäder (Asien), welche als vorübergehende oder aber dauerhafte Einrichtungen konstruiert wurden. Die für den gemeinschaftlichen Gebrauch gedachten Bäder, welche getrennt von den Hütten der Dörfer erbaut wurden, dienten dem Bannen der bösen Geister oder zur Ehrung der Verstorbenen.

Die älteste Badewanne wird auf das Jahr 1700 vor Christus datiert und stammt aus dem Palast von Knossos auf Kreta. Ihre Ähnlichkeit mit aktuellen Badewannen ist, ebenso wie die Ähnlichkeit des damaligen Kanalisationssystems mit heutigen, erstaunlich.

Les indices les plus anciens de salles de bains remontent au troisième millénaire avant Jésus Christ et se divisent en deux catégories : les bains de vapeur (principalement en Europe, en Amérique et en Asie) et les bains froids (Asie), construits à des fins passagères ou permanentes. Les bains d'usage commun, construits au-delà des cabanes et du village, étaient utilisés pour chasser les mauvais esprits et rendre hommage aux défunts.

Les baignoires les plus anciennes datent de 1700 avant Jésus Christ et proviennent du palais de Cnossos en Crète. Leur apparence avec les baignoires d'aujourd'hui est stupéfiante, de même que le système de canalisation des égouts.

La civilisation grecque mentionne l'usage des bains dans plusieurs chapitre de la mythologie. Homère par exemple décrit ses héros mythologiques prenant des

Los indicios más antiguos de baños se remontan al tercer milenio antes de Cristo, y pueden dividirse ya en dos tipos: los baños de vapor (principalmente en Europa, América y Asia) y los baños fríos (Asia), que se establecían en estructuras efímeras o bien en zonas permanentes. Los baños, de uso comunitario, que se construían separados de las cabañas del poblado, se utilizaban para ahuyentar a los malos espíritus o para rendir tributo a los difuntos.

La bañera más antigua data del año 1700 antes de Cristo y proviene del palacio de Cnossos de Creta. Su parecido con las bañeras actuales es asombroso, como también lo es el sistema empleado para los conductos de saneamiento.

La civilización griega incorpora el uso del baño en algunos capítulos mitológicos. Homero por ejemplo, describe a sus héroes mitológicos tomando baños de

the benefits of bathing. Ruins of pre-classical Greek palaces, with areas dedicated to baths, with clay bathtubs and drainage, have been uncovered.

In Roman civilization, the establishment of thermal baths (or shared baths) represented an important advance in the social process, in addition to constituting a major source of health and relaxation. The word thermal, which means 'warm' in Greek, comes from the Greek culture and represents the concept of the arena. Yet, the term was utilized by the Romans to signify the place where tribute was paid to the body by purifying it in steam baths which alternated between cold and hot. Public baths constituted a meeting place and a place of entertainment, and soon became an important public institution. These structures contained rest rooms, exercise rooms, gardens, libraries and museums. Thermal

In der griechischen Kultur findet der Gebrauch des Bades seinen Niederschlag in zahlreichen mythologischen Schriften. Homer beschreibt beispielsweise, wie seine Helden ein warmes Bad nehmen, um ihre Kräfte wiederzuerlangen damit sie ihre Kämpfe fortsetzen können. Die wohltuende Wirkung des Badens wurde auch als Gabe der Götter des Olymps angesehen. Tatsächlich hat man in Griechenland Teile von Palastruinen aus vorklassischer Zeit gefunden, die für Bäder, Badewannen aus gebranntem Lehm und Abflüsse bestimmt waren.

In der römischen Kultur stellte die Einrichtung von Thermen (oder Gemeinschaftsbädern) einen großen Fortschritt in der sozialen Entwicklung dar, und bildete außerdem eine wichtige Grundlage für Gesundheit und Erholung. Das Wort Therme bedeutet „warm" und stammt aus dem Griechischen, und obwohl es

bains d'eau chaude pour reprendre des forces afin de pouvoir poursuivre leurs combats. Le bénéfice des bains est également attribué aux divinités de l'olympe. On découvrit des ruines de palais de la Grèce préclassique ayant des enceintes attribuées à des bains, des baignoires de terre cuite et des égouts.

Dans la civilisation romaine, l'institution des thermes (ou bains publiques) représente un progrès important dans le procès social et constitue une grande source de santé et de relaxation. La notion de thermes vient des Grecs, signifie « chaud » et bien que représentant une arène, elle est utilisée par les romains pour désigner un endroit de culte du corps, où l'on pouvait le purifier dans des piscines et des bains de vapeur, alternant l'eau froide et l'eau chaude. Les bains publics représentaient un point de rencontre et de divertissement devenant ainsi une institution

agua caliente para reponer fuerzas y continuar sus batallas. Los beneficios de los baños se atribuían también a los dioses del Olimpo. Se han encontrado ruinas de palacios de la Grecia preclásica con recintos dedicados al baño con bañeras de tierra cocida y desagües.

En la civilización romana, la institución de las termas (o baños compartidos) representó un importante avance en el proceso social, además de constituir una gran fuente de salud y relajación. La palabra terma significa "caliente" en griego y proviene de la cultura griega, aunque representa el concepto de palestra, término utilizado por los romanos como lugar en donde se rendía tributo al cuerpo purificándolo en piscinas y bañeras de vapor que alternaban agua fría y caliente. Los baños comunitarios constituían además un punto de encuentro y entretenimiento y se convirtieron en una

baths came into being as public buildings where, in principle, there did not exist any formal prohibition disallowing men and women from bathing together. The occurrence of numerous scandals, however, irritated the authorities to the point where they decided to divide the public baths through separation of the sexes. Gradually, society began to draw distinctions between balneae (public baths) and balnea (private baths). More wealthy families had a bath or thermal baths at home. Yet many of them preferred to continue visiting public baths in order to enjoy massages by experts, to perfume themselves with balsam imported from the ends of the Empire, and to

eigentlich für die Vorstellung von einem Gemeinschaftsplatz steht, wurde es von den Römern für den Ort verwendet, an dem sie dem Körper Tribut zollten, indem sie ihn in Schwimmbecken und Dampfbädern reinigten, deren Wasser zwischen kalt und warm wechselte. Die Thermen verkörperten einen Ort des Zusammentreffens und Vergnügens, und entwickelten sich mehr und mehr zu einer wichtigen öffentlichen Institution. Sie umfassten Ruhesäle, Sportanlagen, Gärten und sogar Bibliotheken und Museen. Ursprünglich galten sie als öffentliche Einrichtungen und es gab kein offizielles Verbot, das ein gemeinsames Baden von Männern und Frauen untersagte. Im Laufe der Zeit ereigneten sich jedoch zahlreiche Skandale, die die Obrigkeit in hohem Maße irritierte und sie dazu veranlasste, öffentliche Bäder nach Geschlechtern zu trennen. Nach und nach kristallisierte sich eine Unterscheidung zwischen den sogenannten Heilbädern oder Gemeinschaftsbädern und privaten Bädern heraus. Reichere Familien besaßen Bäder oder Thermenanlagen im eigenen Haus. Nichtsdestotrotz bevorzugten viele Menschen weiterhin den Besuch von

publique importante. Ces édifices conte-
naient des salons de repos, des salles de
gymnastique, des jardins et même des
bibliothèques et des musées. Les thermes naquirent comme édifices publics
où n'existait en principe aucune restric-
tion empêchant les hommes et les fem-
mes de se baigner ensemble. Pourtant,
avec le temps, plusieurs scandales irritè-
rent les autorités qui furent amenées à
diviser les bains et séparer les deux
sexes. Peu à peu, la société fit une distinction entre les bains publics et les
bains privés. Les familles aisées avaient
une salle de bains ou des thermes chez
eux, bien que beaucoup d'entre elles
continuent à fréquenter les bains publics
où elles pouvaient jouir des massages
d'experts, se parfumer avec des baumes
provenant de tous les coins de l'empire
et participer à des débats publics ou autres conversations. A l'apogée de l'empire

importante institución pública. Estos edificios contaban con salones de reposo,
salas de gimnasia, jardines e incluso bi-
bliotecas y museos. Las termas nacieron
como edificios públicos donde en un
principio no existía prohibición formal que
impidiera que hombres y mujeres pudie-
ran bañarse juntos, aunque con el tiempo se sucederían numerosos escándalos
que irritarían a las autoridades hasta di-
vidir los baños públicos y separar ambos
sexos. Poco a poco, la sociedad fue es-
tableciendo distinciones entre los llama-
dos "balneae" o baños públicos y los
"balnea", privados. Las familias más adineradas poseían baño o termas en casa,
aunque muchas de ellas preferían seguir
visitando los edificios públicos para disfrutar de los masajes de los expertos, perfumarse con los bálsamos traídos desde
los confines del imperio y participar en
debates públicos y conversaciones

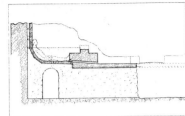

öffentlichen Bädern. Zum einen um in den Genuss fachmännischer Massagen zu kommen oder sich mit den, aus entlegensten Gegenden des Imperiums eingeführten Balsamen einzuparfümieren, zum anderen um an öffentlichen Debatten und dem alltäglichem Geplauder teilzunehmen. Zur Blütezeit des römischen Imperiums benutzte man bereits Toilettenartikel, wie Schüsseln und Spiegel aus Kupfer, Silber oder Glas mit Bleiüberzug. Auch Schmuck und Gegenstände zur Schönheitskosmetik wie Kämme, Haarnadeln, Pinzetten und Gefäße mit Färbemitteln und Salben, viele davon aus dem Orient stammend, wurden hier bereits verwendet. Das Wasser wurde häufig mit Rosenwasser parfümiert und in Fällen von besonderer Raffinesse gebrauchte man Eselsmilch, um die Haut geschmeidig zu machen.

participate in public debates and everyday conservation. At the height of the Roman Empire, bathroom objects such as basins, copper or silver mirrors, and lead-laminated glass were already in use. Also in use were beautification ornaments and objects such as combs, pins, hair needles and vessels for ointments and dyes, many imported from the Orient. The water in private baths could be fragranced with rosewater. In the most refined cases, female donkey milk was used as a way to keep the skin smooth.

Under Roman rule, the Jewish community gradually adopted some of the tendencies of the Empire. Ancestral ablutions were adapted to the form of thermal baths, preserving the public bath as a social custom. Until each community established its own bath, cultural

Das jüdische Volk arrangierte sich unter der römischen Herrschaft nach und nach mit diesen Entwicklungen im Imperium. Die überlieferten Waschrituale wurden den Formen der römischen Therme angepasst und das öffentliche Bad als eine soziale Einrichtung beibehalten. Die kulturellen Unterschiede zwischen Muslimen, Juden und Christen führten

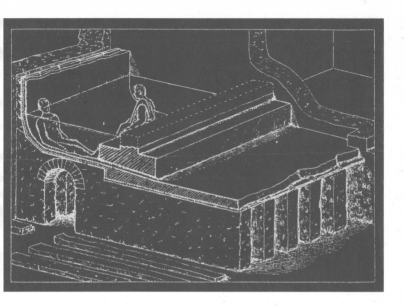

romain, on employait déjà des articles de toilette comme des cuvettes et des miroirs de cuivre, d'argent ou de verre laminé de plomb. On utilisait également des ornements et des objets de décoration tels que des peignes, des pinces, des aiguilles à cheveux, des pots pour les onguents et les colorants, le plus souvent importés d'Orient. On parfumait l'eau des bains privés aux essences de roses et, dans les cas les plus raffinés, on utilisait du lait d'ânesse pour garder une peau lisse.

Le peuple juif se conforma, sous la domination romaine, aux tendances de l'empire. On adapta les ablutions ancestrales à celles des thermes, en conservant les bains publics comme institution sociale. Les différences culturelles firent que les juifs, les musulmans et les chrétiens se partagèrent les installations à des jours différents jusqu'au moment ou

populares. En el apogeo del imperio romano ya se utilizan objetos de aseo como palanganas, espejos de cobre o plata o de cristal laminado con plomo. También se usan ornamentos u objetos de adorno para el embellecimiento como peines, pinzas, agujas de pelo, vasijas para los ungüentos y colorantes, muchos de ellos importados de Oriente. El agua de los baños privados podía perfumarse con agua de rosas y, en los casos más refinados, se utilizaba leche de burra para mantener tersa la piel.

El pueblo judío fue poco a poco adaptándose bajo dominación romana a las tendencias del imperio. Las abluciones ancestrales se ajustaron a la forma de terma romana, pero conservando el baño público como costumbre social. Las diferencias culturales provocaron que judíos, musulmanes y cristianos dividieran las instalaciones en diferentes días hasta

differences necessitated that Jews, Muslims and Christian access the installation on different days. The steam bath, or temazcalli, also extended to pre-Columbian culture and was a feature in the majority of Mesoamerican cities. For Muslims, regulation of body hygiene is laid out in the Koran, where the necessity of washing various parts of the body five times a day for prayer, in addition to other hygienic practices, is established. Arabs in the Orient also preserved the tradition of the hammam (Arabic public baths), with certain modifications with respect to the Roman model. With the spread of Islam, the hammam reached Egypt, Persia, Spain, Morocco and the Muslim countries of Asia and Africa.

While some research affirms that public baths became obsolete in the Renaissance and did not return until the 19th-century, other sources assure us that

dazu, dass die Bäder an verschiedenen Tagen benutzt wurden, bis schließlich jede Kultur ihre eigenen Baderäume erschuf. Das Dampfbad breitete sich auch in der präkolumbianischen Kultur aus und kam in den meisten mexikanischen und mittelamerikanischen Städten unter dem Namen „Temazcalli" zur Anwendung. Für Araber und Muslime ist die Körperhygiene im Koran reglementiert; die fünfmalige Waschung verschiedener Körperteile pro Tag, jeweils vor dem Gebet, ist neben anderen hygienischen Praktiken genau festgelegt. Darüber hinaus hielten die Araber im Orient an der Tradition des Hammam fest, wenngleich auch mit einigen Veränderungen verglichen mit dem römischen Modell. So verbreitete sich das Hammam mit der muslimischen Religion bis nach Ägypten, Persien, Spanien, Marokko sowie in islamische Staaten in Asien und Afrika.

ils créérent chacun leurs propres bains. Le bain de vapeur, appelé également temazcalli, se répandit aussi dans la culture précolombienne ou il était utilisé dans la majorité des villes du Mexique et d'Amérique centrale. Pour les Arabes et les musulmans, l'hygiène corporelle était réglementée dans le Coran, qui prescrivait, au-delà de certaines pratiques hygiéniques, que certaines parties du corps devaient être lavées cinq fois par jour, pour la prière. Les Arabes ont conservés de surcroît en Orient, le hammam en le transformant quelque peu. Le hammam se répandit, avec la religion musulmane jusqu'en Égypte, en Perse, en Espagne, au Maroc et à d'autres états d'Asie et d'Afrique.

Bien que certains ouvrages affirment que les bains publics passèrent de mode à la Renaissance, et ne réapparurent pas avant le 19ième siècle, d'autres sources

que finalmente crearon sus propios espacios.

El baño de vapor o temazcalli se extendió también en la cultura precolombina y se utilizó en la mayoría de las ciudades mexicanas y mesoamericanas. Entre los árabes y musulmanes, por su parte, la higiene corporal está reglamentada en el Corán, que establece que hay que lavar varias partes del cuerpo cinco veces al día –para la oración–, además de otras prácticas higiénicas. Los árabes además conservaron en Oriente el baño con el hammam, aunque con modificaciones respecto al modelo romano. El hammam se propagó con la religión musulmana a Egipto, Persia, España, Marruecos y los países islámicos de Asia y África.

Aunque algunos libros afirman que los baños públicos pasaron de moda en el renacimiento y que no volvieron a surgir hasta el siglo XIX, otras fuentes aseguran

they continued to function in Central and Western Europe. In the English city of Bath, famous for its medicinal waters, the Romans built a spa that was still functioning in high regard throughout the 17th- and 18th-centuries. These public buildings helped promote the neccesity of hygiene, something to which little attention was given. In some cases, bathing was deemed a necessary ritual no more than once a year.

During the Middle Ages, bathing of the whole body was an activity restricted to the more moneyed families. The poverty of the medieval home was such that it lacked adequate places for the practice of hygiene. Pitchers and sponges were used to clean the body. Over time, more simplistic cleansing implements such as brushes and steel buckets came into practice. Later, the domestic apparatus of bourgeois homes were gradually modernized, yet the majority of bourgeois

Auch wenn einige Quellen behaupten, dass öffentliche Bäder in der Renaissance aus der Mode kamen und bis ins 19. Jahrhundert nicht wieder entdeckt wurden, ist es unstrittig, dass sie in Mittel-, West- und Osteuropa weiterhin bestanden. Ein Beispiel ist Bath, eine für ihr heilendes Mineralwasser berühmte englische Stadt, in der die Römer ein Heilbad errichteten, dass noch bis ins 17. und 18. Jahrhundert in Betrieb war und einen exzellenten Ruf genoss. Diese öffentlichen Einrichtungen halfen, die Notwendigkeit von Hygiene stärker bewusst zu machen, die bis dahin sehr wenig Beachtung fand. In einigen Fällen glaubte man sogar, dass Baden als ritueller Akt nur einmal im Jahr notwendig sei.

Während des Mittelalters war das Ganzkörperbad ein den wohlhabenden Familien vorbehaltener Luxus. Die Armut in den mittelalterlichen Haushalten der ländlichen Gegenden war dergestalt, dass keine Räumlichkeiten für die Hygiene vorhanden waren. Hier wurden zur Körperpflege Waschschüsseln und Schwämme benutzt, später kamen auch einfachere Reinigungsgeräte wie Bürsten und Stahlkübel vermehrt zur Anwendung

prétendent qu'ils continuaient à être très appréciés en Europe centrale et de l'Est. Il en est de même pour la cité de Bath, ville anglaise célèbre pour ses eaux minérales et où les romains édifièrent des bains, qui existent encore et qui jouissaient, aux 17ième et 18ième siècles, d'une excellente réputation. Ces édifices publics ont aidé à établir la nécessité de l'hygiène, à laquelle on ne prêtait que peu d'attention. Dans certains cas même, le bain était considéré comme un rite nécessaire qu'une seule fois par année.

Durant le moyen âge, se baigner entièrement était un luxe réservé aux familles aisées. La pauvreté des demeures du moyen âge et le manque d'une place adéquate pour l'hygiène obligeait chacun à se contenter de moyens très rudimentaires. On se lavait avec des cuvettes et des éponges. Avec le temps, les ustensiles les plus simples tels que les peignes et les seaux en métal furent plus utilisés

que siguieron funcionando en el centro y oeste de Europa como en el caso de Bath, ciudad inglesa famosa por sus aguas minerales curativas, donde los romanos construyeron un balneario que continuó funcionando, con excelente reputación, durante los siglos XVII y XVIII. Estos edificios públicos ayudarían a fomentar el necesario uso de la higiene, a la que se prestaba muy poca atención. En algunos casos incluso se consideraba el baño como un rito necesario apenas una vez al año.

Durante la edad media, bañar todo el cuerpo era una acción restringida a las familias más adineradas. Así, la pobreza de la vivienda medieval obligaba a instalarse en un medio rural donde no se disponía de dependencias adecuadas para la higiene. La limpieza corporal se llevaba a cabo con jofainas y esponjas, y poco a poco empezaron a utilizarse accesorios de limpieza simples, como cepillos y cu-

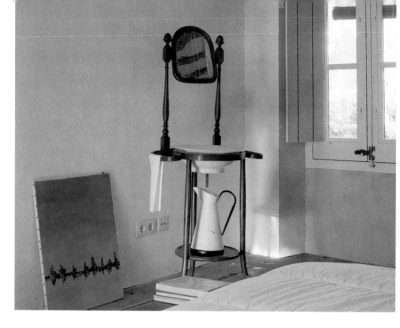

domiciles possessed neither the space nor the infrastructure adequate for equipping a room with bathroom fittings. Gradually, the upper classes began to promote the need for hygiene among the lower classes. Still, the task was not an easy one, given that soap was a luxury product beyond the means of many families. The use of soap also increased, albeit slowly. Mansions and palaces of the period possessed private latrines. The process was slower in rural areas.

During the 16th-, 17th- and 18th-centuries, the general concept of public baths, originally established by Greek and Roman civilizations, disappeared in Europe. Hygiene was thus consigned to portable inventions. In the 18th-century, the bidet was added to the range of already known bathroom fittings. This idiosyncratic object has borne the brunt of constant ridicule up to the present day.

und auch der Gebrauch von Seife erhöhte sich langsam. Mit der Zeit wurden die Haushaltsgeräte in den bürgerlichen Häusern modernisiert, auch wenn die meisten von ihnen nicht über den notwendigen Platz und die Bedingungen verfügten, um sie mit allen notwendigen Gerätschaften für ein eigenes Badezimmer auszustatten. Stück für Stück überzeugten die Oberschichten die unteren Klassen von der Notwendigkeit einer besseren Hygiene, obwohl dies angesichts der Tatsache, dass Seife ein sehr teures Produkt war, das sich nicht alle Familien leisten konnten, keine leichte Aufgabe war. Große Villen und Schlösser besaßen zudem separate einfache Toiletteneinrichtungen. In den ländlichen Gegenden verzögerte sich der gesamte Entwicklungsprozess jedoch um einiges.

Im Europa des 16., 17. und 18. Jahrhunderts verschwand der allgemeine

et l'usage du savon augmenta lentement. Plus tard, les maisons bourgeoises furent modernisées avec divers ustensiles, bien que la majorité d'entre elles ne disposaient ni de la place, ni de l'infrastructure permettant d'avoir une salle de bains avec tout son équipement. Peu à peu les classes supérieures persuadèrent les classes moins privilégies de la nécessité d'une meilleure hygiène. Ce n'était pas chose facile, le savon était une denrée cher, que tout le monde ne pouvait pas s'offrir. Les grandes maisons particulières et les châteaux avaient des latrines privées. Dans les régions rurales, ce progrès ne se répandit que très lentement.

En Europe des 16ième, 17ième et 18ième siècles, le concept général de bains publiques instauré principalement par les civilisations grecques et romaines disparut. Cela était dû à l'invention des

bos de acero, y paulatinamente aumentó el uso del jabón. Posteriormente las casas burguesas fueron modernizando sus utensilios domésticos, aunque la mayoría no disponía de espacio ni infraestructura para ocupar una habitación con todos los enseres del baño. Progresivamente, las clases superiores fueron propagando la necesidad de mayor higiene a las menos favorecidas, aunque no fue tarea fácil, puesto que el jabón era un producto muy caro que no podían conseguir todas las familias. Las grandes mansiones y castillos de la época contaban además con letrinas particulares. El proceso fue más lento en las zonas rurales.

En Europa, durante los siglos XVI, XVII y XVIII desaparece el concepto general de baño público, por lo que la higiene queda relegada a los elementos portátiles inventados. A los sanitarios ya conocidos se incorpora el bidé (aparece en el siglo XVIII). Aparece como pieza singular, vícti-

The first models were portable and made of porcelain, the same material used for sinks and urinals during this period. Although not typical of this particular historical moment, certain palaces began to be equipped with rooms dedicated exclusively to hygienic functions.

In America, pre-Hispanic cities experienced an evolution parallel to that of European culture, although with certain delays. The Spanish introduced portable objects and meager bathing systems in progressive but very slow fashion.

With the arrival of the modern age, dwellings came to reflect the concept of intimacy, and the currency of the idea of the home as an open public space diminished. As a fruit of medieval bourgeois society, the home took on the identity of single-family space, and its articulation changed radically.

In the middle of the 19th-century, the home was organized according to its

Grundgedanke von öffentlichen Bädern und das Bezeichnende in dieser Zeit war die Weiterentwicklung hygienischer Elemente. Im 18. Jahrhundert wird das Bidet den bereits bekannten sanitären Einrichtungen hinzugefügt. Es handelte sich dabei um einen außergewöhnlichen Gegenstand, der damals Anlass zu viel Spott gab. Die ersten Modelle waren tragbare Objekte aus Porzellan, dem gleichen Material, das man zu dieser Zeit für Waschbecken und Nachtöpfe verwendete. Auch wenn es nicht signifikant für die Gesellschaft dieser Epoche ist, begann man in einigen Palästen erste Räumlichkeiten einzurichten, die ausschließlich dem Baden dienten.

In Amerika fand mit gewisser Verzögerung eine parallele Entwicklung zur europäischen Badekultur statt und durch die Spanier wurden tragbare Geräte und behelfsmäßige Bädersysteme eingeführt.

Mit dem Beginn des modernen Zeitalters spiegelte sich in den Häusern die Idee der Intimität wider. Die Vorstellung vom Haus als einem allgemeinen und öffentlichen Raum tritt mehr und mehr in den Hintergrund. Die gesammelten Erfahrungen der Bourgeoisie führten zu der

nouveaux éléments destinés à l'hygiène. Aux sanitaires, déjà connus à l'époque, vînt s'ajouter le bidet qui apparaît au 18ième siècle. Il s'agit d'une pièce particulière qui fût toujours victime de commentaires ironiques, qui n'ont pas changés de nos jours. Les premiers modèles étaient des objets portables en porcelaine, matériel également utilisé à l'époque pour les lavabos et les pots de chambre. Bien que n'étant pas représentatif pour la société de l'époque, on commença, dans certains palais, à consacrer une pièce séparée à la salle de bains.

En Amérique, on remarqua avec un certain retard une évolution parallèle à celle la culture européenne. Les Espagnols introduisent des éléments portables et progressivement, bien que beaucoup plus lentement, les premiers systèmes de bains très précaires.

ma constante de ironías. Los primeros modelos eran objetos portátiles de porcelana, el mismo material que utilizaban para los lavabos y orinales de la época. Aunque no es representativo de la sociedad del momento, en algunos palacios se empieza a dedicar estancias exclusivas para los baños.

En América, las ciudades prehispánicas sufren una evolución paralela a la cultura europea, aunque con cierto retraso; los españoles introducen los utensilios y elementos portátiles y los precarios sistemas de baño.

Con la edad moderna, la vivienda adopta el concepto de intimidad, y se aleja de la idea de la casa como espacio abierto y público. Fruto de las experiencias de la sociedad burguesa de la edad media, se asume el concepto de vivienda como espacio único para la familia, y su distribución cambia radicalmente.

usefulness. Attitudes towards the role of bathrooms thus took another turn. Society was concerned with guarding against the spread of contagious disease, and the most efficacious way to combat them was through commitment to better hygiene. Mass showers were made available to the poorest classes. Around 1870, the prevailing practice was to disinfect kitchens and bathrooms, a consequence of new research attributing the cause of numerous diseases to germs. Bathrooms became independent and isolated from the other rooms. The objective was to have exceedingly hygienic areas with decorative colors and materi-

Ansicht, dass das Heim ein ausschließlich für die Familie bestimmter Bereich sei, und seine räumliche Anordnung wandelte sich radikal.

In der Mitte des 19. Jahrhunderts wurde die Planung eines Hauses an der Zweckmäßigkeit orientiert und der Gebrauch des Bades bekam somit einen anderen Stellenwert. Die Gesellschaft musste der Ausbreitung von ansteckenden Krankheiten entgegentreten und der beste Weg zur Bekämpfung war der Einsatz für eine bessere Hygiene. Zunächst wurden für die untersten sozialen Schichten öffentliche Duschen eingeführt, um 1870 dann als Konsequenz der neuen Forschungen, die zahlreiche Krankheiten auf die Verbreitung von Keimen zurückführten, zielte das allgemeine Bemühen auf die Notwendigkeit der Desinfektion von Küchen und Bädern ab, und die Bäder wurden eigenständig und von den übrigen Räumen isoliert eingerichtet. Ziel war es, größtmögliche Hygiene und Sauberkeit zu erlangen, was die Räume auch in ihren Farben und Dekorationen widerspiegelten.

Mit dem Beginn der industriellen Revolution standen den Reicheren erste

A l'arrivée des temps modernes s'ajoute la notion d'intimité. On s'éloigne de l'idée de la maison en tant que lieu ouvert et public. Fruit des expériences de la bourgeoisie du moyen âge, on reprend le concept de logement, comme étant un espace uniquement réservé à la famille, ce qui entraîna un changement radical de sa conception.

Dès le milieu du 19ième siècle, on répartit les pièces selon des critères dictés par la raison et l'utilisation du bain prit une autre position. La société devait lutter contre des maladies contagieuses et la meilleure forme de les combattre était d'améliorer les conditions d'hygiène. Pour les classes les plus défavorisées, on instaure des douches publiques. Aux alentours de 1870, en conséquence à de nouvelles recherches attribuant aux germes un grand nombre de maladies, on estime qu'il est nécessaire de désinfecter les cuisines et les salles de bains.

A mediados del siglo XIX se distribuye la casa en función de su practicidad y el uso del baño toma otra dirección. La sociedad debe luchar contra enfermedades contagiosas, y la mejor forma de combatirlas es apostar por una mayor higiene. Se utilizan duchas populares para las clases más desfavorecidas y, con la llegada de la revolución industrial, los más adinerados disponen de las primeras tecnologías que mecanizan el baño. A mitad de siglo, las viviendas burguesas dedican un espacio para las prácticas higiénicas, con aparatos diseñados para canalizar el suministro del agua. Poco después se venderá el agua caliente a domicilio y se empezará a poner de moda el baño a la carta: baños de azahar, de miel, de esencia de rosas ... Hacia el año 1870, y a consecuencia de las nuevas investigaciones que atribuyen a los gérmenes numerosas enfermedades, impera la necesidad de desinfectar cocinas y baños, por lo

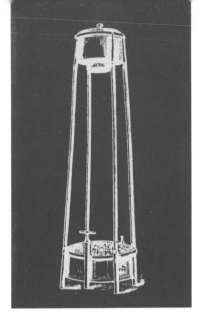

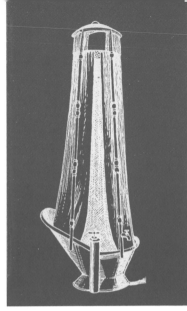

als that favored an image of immaculateness. With the advent of the Industrial Revolution, the rich made use of the first technologies to mechanize the bathroom. At mid-century, middle-class homes possessed a space for practicing hygiene, with apparatus designed to channel water supply. Not long after, hot water could be purchased for use in the home. As a result, personalized baths (orange or lemon blossom baths, honey baths, rose essence baths) became fashionable.

At the end of the 19th century, the room dedicated exclusively to hygiene came to be used by all members of the family, though not simultaneously. Simple woodwork was replaced by decorated glazed tile and decorative elements. With the passage of time and technological advances, more prominence was given to the formal design of bathrooms than

Technologien zur Verfügung, die das Bad mechanisierten. Gegen Mitte des Jahrhunderts besaßen bürgerliche Wohnhäuser für die Körperpflege einen Raum mit Vorrichtungen für die Regulierung der Wasserversorgung. Kurz danach wurde warmes Wasser für die private Benutzung verkauft und infolge dessen kam das Baden „à la carte" mit Orangenblüten, Honig und Rosenessenzen in Mode.

Gegen Ende des 19. Jahrhunderts wurde der bis dahin ausschließlich der Hygiene dienende Raum weiterentwickelt. Einfache Schreinerarbeiten wurden von bemalten Fliesen und anderen dekorativen Elementen abgelöst. Mit dem Voranschreiten der Zeit und dem Aufkommen neuer Technologien, wurde dem formalen Design des Bades eine größere Bedeutung als nur die der rein praktischen Funktion zugesprochen. Neue Modelle und Formen, innovative Materialien und

De ce fait, ces pièces obtiennent une indépendance et viennent séparées des autres chambres afin de garantir une hygiène extrême. Les couleurs et les matériaux de décoration aidant à en donner une image immaculée.

A la fin du 19ième siècle, les pièces réservées uniquement à l'hygiène évoluent. Les travaux de menuiserie sont remplacés par des carrelages peints ainsi que d'autres éléments décoratifs. Peu à peu, avec les années et l'apparition des nouvelles technologies, la salle de bains donne plus d'importance au design des formes et moins aux fonctions purement pratiques. On introduit de nouveaux modèles, de nouvelles formes, des matériaux et revêtements originaux et des lavabos et autres sanitaires très innovateurs.

La salle de bains dite « européenne », est une pièce de grande dimension, dans que estos espacios adquieren independencia y se aislan de las otras habitaciones para conformar espacios sumamente higiénicos, con colores y materiales en su decoración que ayudan a propiciar una imagen inmaculada.

A finales de siglo XIX, la habitación dedicada exclusivamente a la higiene es utilizada por todos los miembros de la familia, aunque de forma separada. Los sencillos trabajos de ebanistería van siendo reemplazados por azulejos decorados y ornamentos. El llamado cuarto de baño europeo es un recinto de grandes dimensiones, en muchos casos un dormitorio remodelado en el que se separa el retrete de la zona de baño. En la misma época surge el modelo americano, de dimensiones más reducidas, concebido como un espacio privado con todos los elementos higiénicos distribuidos en un mismo ambiente. Poco a

to their purely practical function. New models and forms, creative materials and coverings, and innovative sinks and toilets were introduced as fresh possibilities for the modern bathroom.

The so-called "European bathroom" is a large space, in many cases a remodeled bedroom, in which the lavatory is separated from the bathing area. During the same period, the American model emerged. It was smaller than its European counterpart and conceived as a private space with all hygienic elements distributed in a single environment.

Beschichtungen sowie neuartige Waschbecken- und Toilettenformen wurden für das moderne Badezimmer eingeführt.

Das so genannte „europäische Badezimmer" ist ein groß dimensionierter Raum, in vielen Fällen ein umgebautes Schlafzimmer, in dem die Toilette vom eigentlichen Badbereich getrennt ist. Zur selben Zeit trat das „amerikanische Modell" auf. Es ist kleiner als sein europäisches Gegenstück und wird als ein privater Raum verstanden, in dem alle der Hygiene dienenden Elemente in einem Zimmer vereint sind.

The Bathtub and Shower: Examples of Evolution

Die Entwicklung am Beispiel der Badewanne und Dusche

Today's bathroom fittings are merely updated models of the implements already being used by our forebears, who were motivated by the need to meet

Die sanitären Einrichtungen, die heute in unseren Bädern zum Einsatz kommen, sind im Grunde nur neue Modelle jener Ausstattungen, die bereits unsere

beaucoup de cas une chambre à coucher transformée dans laquelle on sépare les toilettes du reste de la pièce. Le modèle « américain » de son côté apparaît également. Il est plus petit que son pendant européen et est conçu comme pièce séparée dans laquelle tous les éléments déservant l'hygiène sont réunis.

La baignoire et la douche comme exemples de l'évolution

Les sanitaires employés dans les salles de bains actuelles sont uniquement les modèles actualisé des éléments que nos ancêtres utilisaient, poussés par le besoin de couvrir leurs nécessités hygiéniques et leurs rituels les plus consacrés. Il est curieux d'observer des baignoires qui remontent à l'an 2000 avant J.C., date de son origine dans les civilisations d'Asie mineure et de l'Est

poco, con el paso de los años y el avance de las nuevas tecnologías, el cuarto de baño concede más protagonismo al diseño de sus formas que a la función puramente práctica. Se introducen nuevos modelos y formas, originales materiales y revestimientos e innovadores modelos de lavamanos y sanitarios para el nuevo cuarto de baño.

La bañera y la ducha como ejemplos de evolución

Los sanitarios que empleamos en el baño actual son sólo nuevos modelos de los instrumentos que ya utilizaban nuestros antepasados, movidos por el empeño de cubrir sus necesidades higiénicas y sus rituales más consagrados. Es curioso observar enseres muy parecidos a los que utilizamos en la actualidad y que datan del año 2000 antes de Cristo, fecha

both sanitary and the most consecrated ritualistic demands. It is striking to observe fittings, very similar to ones we use today, dating back to the year 2000 B.C., the date of birth of the bathtub in the civilizations of Asia Minor and the Eastern Mediterranean. Terracotta bathtubs supported by walls required the bather to tuck in his or her legs in order to fit. Vessels filled with water were used to wet the body. Fireplaces, likely used to heat water, have been found close to the tubs. Minoan bathtubs have the appearance of a sarcophagus, while Greek baths tend to be longer and more spacious. Some were capable of holding several persons.

The Roman period saw the evolution of public baths. Consequently, private baths became less common. Some baths consisted of marble, onyx, silver and bronze while others—so-called solium baths—permitted bathing while

Vorfahren benutzten. Es ist erstaunlich, wenn man Apparaturen sieht, die aus dem Jahre 2000 v. Chr. stammen, dem Zeitpunkt des Auftretens der Badewanne in Kleinasien und dem östlichen Mittelmeerraum, und diese sich von den heute von uns verwendeten kaum unterscheiden. Die ersten Badewannen waren Modelle aus Terracotta, die von Mauergestein umgeben waren, und in denen der Benutzer seine Beine anziehen musste. Mit Wasser gefüllte Gefäße dienten dazu, ihn mit Wasser zu übergießen. In der Nähe der Badewannen wurden Feuerstellen gefunden, mit deren Hilfe vermutlich das Wasser erhitzt wurde. Die Badewannen der minoischen Kultur ähnelten Sarkophagen, während die griechischen Modelle dazu tendierten, breiter und länger zu sein und mitunter sogar mehrere Personen aufnehmen konnten.

In der römischen Epoche entwickelte sich die Idee der Gemeinschaftsbäder und verdrängte die privaten Bäder. Einige Bäder waren aus Marmor, Onyx oder sogar aus Silber und Bronze errichtet, während andere, die sogenannten solium-Bäder, das Sitzen während des Badens erlaubten. Letztere waren eine Art

de la Méditerranée, qui ne se différencient guère de celles employées de nos jours. Elles apparaissent comme modèles en terre cuite, sont soutenues par des murs et leurs utilisateurs doivent replier leurs jambes et utiliser des pots remplis d'eau pour s'asperger le corps. A côté des baignoires se trouvaient des foyers destinée probablement à chauffer l'eau. Les baignoires de la culture minoïque avaient l'aspect d'un sarcophage, tandis que celles de la culture grecque étaient plus grandes et plus larges, offrant parfois de la place à plusieurs personnes.

A l'époque romaine, l'évolution des bains communs supplantent les baignoires privées. Certains d'entre eux étaient en marbre, en onyx, en argent ou en bronze, d'autres permettaient parfois de se baigner assis et s'appelaient, alors, solium. Ils furent les précurseurs des douches assises qui, beaucoup plus tard,

de origen de la bañera en las civilizaciones de Asia Menor y del este del Mediterráneo. Surgen como modelos de terracota, apoyadas en muros, en las que su ocupante debía encoger las piernas y utilizar vasijas para dejarse caer el agua por el cuerpo. Cerca de las bañeras se han encontrado chimeneas, en las que debían de calentar el agua. Las bañeras de la cultura minoica tienen aspecto de sarcófago, mientras que en la cultura griega tienden a ser más amplias y alargadas, algunas con capacidad para varias personas.

En la época romana el concepto de baño común evolucionó y se arrinconaron las bañeras individuales. Algunas eran de mármol, ónice e incluso de plata y bronce, y otras, las llamadas solium, permitían bañarse sentado, adelantándose al invento del sillón-ducha que, mucho más tarde, en 1859, Griffith presentaría como

sitting down. The latter were a kind of precursor to the shower-seat, which many years later, in 1859, Griffith would introduce as a great social advance. In the Middle Ages, Arabic baths appropriated to a large extent the infrastructure of the Roman bath. At the same time, Arabs also used permanent built-in models as well as portable versions. The portable bath resembled a large wooden barrel and could be situated in any part of the house. Whole families, along with guests, would bathe in it together. Palaces and castles had huge bathtubs made of marble and porcelain. In the 18th-century, copper, onyx and metal were commonly used materials. The search for ways to reduce water consumption in the 19th-century favored showering in place of bathing. Nonetheless, at mid-century the prosperity of some cities resulted in the resurgence of

Vorläufer der Sitzbadewanne, die erst viele Jahre später, 1859, von Griffith als eine große soziale Errungenschaft eingeführt wurde. Im Mittelalter wurden in den römischen Badeanlagen weitenteils arabische Bäder eingerichtet. Ferner waren in privaten Haushalten auch fest installierte und tragbare Modelle in Gebrauch. Die tragbaren Wannen ähnelten einem großen Holzfass, in dem eine ganze Familie, sogar zusammen mit ihren Gästen, baden konnte, ganz gleich in welchem Raum des Hauses. Paläste und Schlösser waren mit Badewannen aus Marmor und Porzellan in monumentalen Formen ausgestattet. Die gebräuchlichsten Materialien während des 18. Jahrhunderts waren Kupfer, Onyx und Metall. Im 19. Jahrhunderts führte die Suche nach Möglichkeiten zur Reduzierung des Wasserverbrauchs dazu, dass der Gebrauch der Dusche gegenüber dem der Badewanne

en 1859, furent présentées comme grand progrès social par un certain Griffith. Au moyen âge, les bains arabes reprirent en grande partie l'infrastructure romaine. On employait également des modèles encastrés ou portables ressemblant à de grands tonneaux de bois et dans lesquels toute la famille de même que les invités pouvait prendre place. Ils pouvaient être placés à n'importe quel endroit de la maison. Les palais et les châteaux avaient des baignoires de marbre ou de porcelaine de taille monumentale. Au 18ième siècle, elles étaient en cuivre, en onyx ou en métal. Au 19ième siècle, on chercha à créer des modèles plus petits permettant d'économiser l'eau, favorisant la douche au détriment de la baignoire, bien que vers le milieu du siècle la prospérité de certaines villes fit renaître son usage et lui permit de revenir à la mode. A la fin du 19ième

un gran avance social. En la edad media, los baños árabes utilizaron gran parte de la infraestructura romana, aunque también se usaron modelos fijos empotrados y modelos portátiles, parecidos a un gran tonel de madera, en donde se bañaban juntos todos los miembros de la familia y sus invitados, en cualquier parte de la casa. Los palacios y castillos incorporaban bañeras de mármol y porcelana de formas monumentales. El cobre, el ónice y el metal son materiales utilizados durante el siglo XVIII. En los baños del siglo XIX influye la búsqueda de formas que reduzcan el consumo del agua, favoreciendo el uso de la ducha en detrimento de la bañera, aunque a mediados de siglo, con el bienestar de algunas ciudades, resurgen atractivos modelos de bañera que volverán a poner de moda este tipo de sanitario. A finales del XIX, con el concepto de baño como único espacio, la

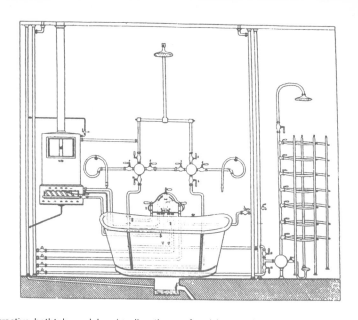

attractive bathtub models, signaling the return to fashion of this bathroom accoutrement. In line with the late 19th-century concept of the bathroom as a unified space, the bathtub jettisoned its portable character and was definitively incorporated into the bathroom. New wood and painted metal models emerged. The beginning of the 20th-century witnessed the appearance of glazed porcelain bathtubs as an effective way of staving off rust. Also seen were iron bathtubs with an enamelled porcelain layer. Over the years, models built into the floor and large bathtubs have made a comeback. The passage of time has also brought the utilization of other materials, such as plastic.

During many centuries, showering was our forebears' primary form of purification. It consisted in the pouring of water over the body, which then fell to the floor.

favorisiert wurde. Nichtsdestotrotz brachte gegen Mitte des Jahrhunderts der Wohlstand einiger Städten eine Wiederbelebung des Interesses an attraktiven Badewannentypen mit sich, sodass diese Badezimmerausstattungen wieder in Mode kamen. Am Ende dieses Jahrhunderts führte die Idee vom Bad als einem eigenständigen Raum zur Aufgabe des Modelles der tragbaren Badewanne und diese wird endgültig fester Bestandteil des Badezimmers. Neue Varianten aus Holz und bemaltem Metall kamen auf den Markt. Zu Beginn des zwanzigsten Jahrhunderts kamen Wannen mit Porzellanüberzug oder aus Email auf, die eine optimale Lösung zur Verhinderung von Rostbildung darstellten. Im Laufe der Jahre erlebten im Boden eingebaute Modelle sowie Wannen von großem Ausmaß eine Renaissance und es wurden neue Materialien wie zum Beispiel das Plastik verwendet.

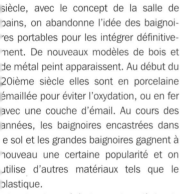

siècle, avec le concept de la salle de bains, on abandonne l'idée des baignoires portables pour les intégrer définitivement. De nouveaux modèles de bois et de métal peint apparaissent. Au début du 20ième siècle elles sont en porcelaine émaillée pour éviter l'oxydation, ou en fer avec une couche d'émail. Au cours des années, les baignoires encastrées dans le sol et les grandes baignoires gagnent à nouveau une certaine popularité et on utilise d'autres matériaux tels que le plastique.

La douche a été durant des siècles la forme la plus courante à nos ancêtre de se laver. Elle consistait à se verser de l'eau sur le corps. Les cultures anciennes réservaient déjà un emplacement à la douche, doté d'un écoulement et d'un plateau de douche en pierres. Bien que délogée par la baignoire pendant des décennies, son usage fut redécouvert à des fins thérapeutiques. Jusqu'au 19ième siècle, elle représentait une très bonne

bañera abandona su carácter portátil y se integra definitivamente en el cuarto de baño. Surgen nuevos modelos de madera y de metal pintado. A principios del siglo XX aparecen con un esmalte de porcelana, solución óptima para evitar la oxidación, y también bañeras de hierro con una capa de porcelana esmaltada. Con el paso de los años se recuperan los modelos empotrados en el suelo y los de gran tamaño, y se utilizarán otros materiales como el plástico.

La ducha fue durante muchos siglos la principal forma de purificación de nuestros antepasados, y consistía en derramar agua por el cuerpo hasta caer al suelo. Las culturas más antiguas ya destinaban un espacio a la ducha, con un sumidero para el agua, e incluso colocaban piedras talladas como platos de ducha. Aunque el uso de la ducha cayó en detrimento de la bañera durante muchas

In the most ancient civilizations, a space was already being set aside for showering, with a drain and even cut stones to serve as shower bases. Throughout many decades the shower fell into disuse and bathing took its place. Showering made a return, however, as a therapy to combat disease. Around the 19th-century, it became an effective option available to members of lower social classes who lacked private means of hygiene. In the most densely populated urban areas,

Die Dusche war viele Jahrhunderte hindurch die gebräuchlichste Reinigungsform unserer Vorfahren und bestand in dem Ausschütten von Wasser über den Körper, das dann auf den Boden lief. Die ältesten Kulturen hatten für die Dusche bereits einen separaten Platz, mit einem Abfluss und einer Duschwanne aus behauenen Steinen. Obwohl der Gebrauch der Dusche während vieler Jahrzehnte durch die Badewanne in den Hintergrund gedrängt wurde, besann man sich später wieder auf sie als eine Therapie gegen Krankheiten. Bis ins neunzehnte Jahrhundert stellte sie eine gute Lösung für sozial schwächere Schichten dar, die selbst nicht über geeignete Möglichkeiten der Körperhygiene verfügten. In den am dichtesten besiedelten Stadtvierteln wurden sanitäre Duschen eingerichtet, um Infektionskrankheiten zu bekämpfen. In den bürgerlichen Familien wurden zu Duschen umgebaute Sitzbadewannen verwendet.

Viel später begann dann die kommerzielle Vermarktung von Duschkabinen, welche die Hersteller mit der Betonung

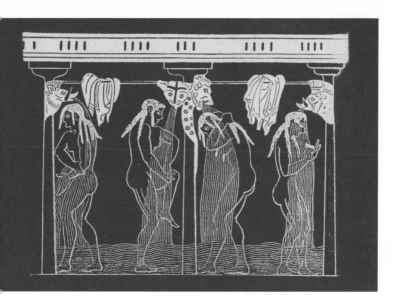

olution pour les gens n'ayant pas de grands moyens, d'accéder à une certaine hygiène. Dans les quartiers les plus peuplés, la douche permettait de combattre es maladies infectieuses. Les familles bourgeoises avaient leur propres douches instalées dans des baignoires transformées.

Plus tard, on commença à commercialiser les cabines de douche, que les fabricants vendaient en prisant leur effet e massage thérapeutique. Pendant uelques décennies, les douches remlacèrent les baignoires, étant considéées comme plus hygiéniques et plus conomiques. Peu après, pourtant, les aignoires-douches firent leur apparition ombinant les deux. Aujourd'hui avec les ouveautés techniques, les baignoires odernes et les cabines de douche ont ne série de dispositifs qui en font de rais robots de l'hygiène.

décadas, volvió a recuperarse como terapia para las enfermedades. Hacia el siglo XIX resultó una buena solución para las clases sociales que no poseían medios propios de higiene. Los barrios urbanos más densamente poblados utilizaban las duchas sanitarias para combatir las enfermedades infecciosas. Las familias burguesas disponían de duchas domésticas, adaptaciones de bañeras de asiento.

Más tarde empezaron a comercializarse cabinas con ducha, que los fabricantes vendían subrayando los beneficios de sus masajes terapéuticos. En algunas décadas del siglo XIX las duchas llegaron a sustituir a las bañeras, al ser consideradas más higiénicas y económicas, aunque pronto apareció el modelo bañera-ducha, que unió en uno ambos sanitarios. En la actualidad, con las últimas innovaciones tecnológicas, la bañera moderna y las cabinas de ducha introducen

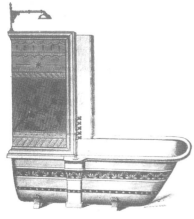

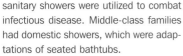

sanitary showers were utilized to combat infectious disease. Middle-class families had domestic showers, which were adaptations of seated bathtubs.

Later, shower stalls began to be commercialized as manufacturers underscored the benefits of massage therapy. During some decades of the 19th-century, showers came to substitute baths as a more hygienic and economical alternative. But soon the bathtub-shower appeared, joining the two implements in one. Today, the latest innovative technology has resulted in bathtubs and shower stalls with a series of mechanical devices that make these fittings into literal robots of hygiene.

The modern bath

New tendencies in the concept of baths lean toward spaces which are intimate

der Vorteile einer therapeutischen Massage verkauften. Während einiger Jahrzehnte des 19. Jahrhunderts ersetzte die Dusche die Badewanne, weil sie als die hygienischere und ökonomischere Variante angesehen wurde. Kurz danach jedoch kam das Modell der Duschbadewanne auf den Markt, die beide Vorrichtungen miteinander verband. Heutzutage haben die neuesten technischen Errungenschaften zu Badewannen und Duschkabinen geführt, die mit einer ganzen Reihe neuer Mechanismen ausgestattet sind und sie so in regelrechte Hygieneroboter verwandelt haben.

Das moderne Badezimmer

Die neuen Tendenzen in der Konzeption von Badezimmern bevorzugen Räume die sowohl intim als auch für die ganze Familie geschaffen sind. Das Design, natürliche Materialien sowie Zubehörteile den neuesten Technologien haben dazu geführt, das dieser Ort sich zu einer

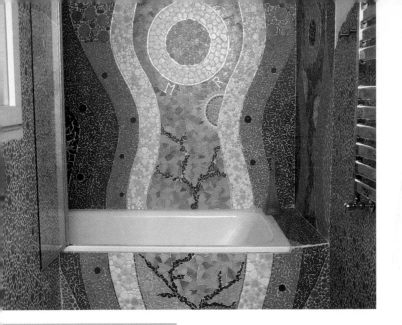

Les salles de bains d'aujourd'hui

es nouvelles tendances plaident pour
ne salle de bains intime, destinée pour-
ant à toute la famille. Le design, des
matériaux naturels et des accessoires de
ernière technologie la transformèrent en
n lieu utile et personnel à la fois. Dans
a société actuelle, la salle de bains
onstitue un espace voué à la relaxation,
u repos et au bien être et en font l'une
es pièces les plus importantes de la
maison. Ce nouveau concept ne cor-
espond plus à l'idée d'une pièce uniquement consacrée à l'hygiène. En ce moment, la tendance est plutôt à agrandir
es salles de bains, s'agissant d'une piè-
e où l'on est supposé passer plus de
emps qu'avant. Les petites tailles dans
es sanitaires ne sont employées que
our les toilettes et les bidets (ceux-ci
tant plus utilisés dans certains pays que

una serie de dispositivos que las convierten en auténticos robots de la higiene.

El baño en la actualidad

Las nuevas tendencias en el baño abogan por estancias íntimas, aunque
abiertas a toda la familia, con diseños,
materiales naturales y accesorios de última tecnología que lo convierten en un
espacio útil y muy personal. En la sociedad actual, el cuarto de baño constituye un espacio dedicado a la relajación y al relax, y configura el centro del
bienestar y una de las habitaciones
más importantes de la vivienda. Este
nuevo concepto desplaza la idea de baño como habitación con funciones puramente higiénicas. En la actualidad, el
tamaño del baño tiende a aumentar,
puesto que se trata de una habitación
diseñada para dedicar mucho más

yet available to the whole family. Designs, natural materials and the most cutting-edge accessories have converted this area into both an utilitarian and personal space. In today's society, the bathroom is an area dedicated to rest and relaxation. It constitutes the center of well-being of the home and is thus one of the most important rooms in the house. This new concept displaces the idea of the bath as a room whose function is limited to hygiene. Nowadays, bathroom size tends to be large, reflecting the fact that much more time is spent in bathrooms than before. Smaller dimensions apply solely to the lavatory and bidet (the latter more common in some countries than in others). As opposed to bathrooms of the past, today's bathroom occupies an area replete with light and is one of the most meticulously fitted out rooms in the house.

Modern bathrooms embody pure clean designs and are reminiscent of oriental or Zen-style baths. While eastern influence

nützlichen gleichzeitig aber auch seh persönlichen Raum gewandelt hat. In de heutigen Gesellschaft stellt das Bad ei nen Raum dar, der der Ruhe und Ent spannung dient. Er wird so zum Mittel punkt des Wohlbefindens und zu einer der wichtigsten Räume der Wohnun, überhaupt. Dieses neue Konzept ersetz die Vorstellung vom Bad als einem Raur mit einer ausschließlich hygienische Funktion. Man geht heute dazu über, di Größe des Badezimmers zu erweitern, d es sich um einen Ort handelt, an der man erheblich mehr Zeit als früher ver bringt. Die kleinsten Maße verwende man nur noch beim Wasserklosett und beim Bidet (letzteres wird in einigen Län dern mehr genutzt als in anderen). Ir Gegensatz zu früheren Zeiten, befinde sich das Bad heute an einem Platz m viel Licht und es ist zu einem der be sten ausgestatteten Räume des Hause geworden.

Die neuen Bäder zeichnet ein klares un reines Design aus, das an orientalisch

dans d'autres). Contrairement au passé, la salle de bains est placée à un endroit très lumineux et est l'une des pièces les mieux équipée de la maison.

Les nouvelles salles de bains ont un design pur et net rappelant les bains orientaux et de style Zen. Il est certain que les influences orientales ont modifié une grande partie des coutumes domestiques de salles de bains occidentales, de même que les orientaux ont intégré des habitudes occidentales aux leurs. La salle de bains de style japonais (bain public) s'adapte à nos nécessités familières. Aujourd'hui, cet endroit joue le rôle que tenaient à un certain moment le vestiaire, la chambre d'enfants ou de toilette. Nous avons adopté des traditions millénaires de la culture orientale tel que le Feng Shui, qui est la science de définir

tiempo que antes. Las medidas mínimas se aplican únicamente al inodoro y al bidé (más utilizado en unos países que en otros). El baño se sitúa en un lugar repleto de luz, a diferencia del pasado, y es uno de los espacios más equipados de la casa.

Los nuevos baños incorporan diseños puros y limpios, que recuerdan los baños orientales o de estilo zen. Es cierto que las influencias orientales han modificado gran parte de las costumbres domésticas del baño occidental, de la misma forma que los orientales han incorporado a su propia cultura hábitos de Occidente. El baño de estilo japonés (el baño común) se adapta a nuestras necesidades familiares. Hoy en día este espacio se ajusta a las funciones que en otros tiempos desempeña-

has resulted in significant modifications to occidental domestic bath customs, oriental culture has also adopted certain western habits. The Japanese-style bath (the public bath), for example, has assimilated our domestic necessities. Today, this space is the site for activity which in other times took place in dressing rooms, children's rooms and boudoirs. From oriental culture, on the other hand, we have appropriated such thousand-year-old traditions as Feng Shui, the ancient Chinese wisdom of location. Feng Shui focuses on redistribution of the home—including the bathroom—with the aim of achieving harmony and equilibrium. According to this tradition, our vital energy, or Chi, should flow harmoniously through all rooms. Given that the bathroom is the site of drains and open fittings, this vital energy finds easy escape in this quarter of the home. It is therefore imperative that the bathroom remain closed as much as

Bäder oder auch an den Zen-Stil erinnert. Es ist gesichert, dass orientalische Einflüsse zu einer starken Veränderung der häuslichen Gewohnheiten im westlichen Bad geführt haben, in gleicher Weise wie die orientalische Kultur einige Gepflogenheiten der westlichen Welt übernommen hat. So passt sich das Bad im japanischen Stil (das Gemeinschaftsbad) zum Beispiel unseren familiären Bedürfnissen an. Heute hat dieser Raum Aufgaben, die in anderen Zeiten von Ankleidezimmern, Kinderzimmern und sogar Toiletten übernommen wurden. Von der asiatischen Kultur haben wir uns tausendjährige Traditionen wie das Feng Shui zu Eigen gemacht, das alte Wissen Chinas über die Positionierung der Einrichtung, welche den Wohnraum (inklusive des Badezimmers) mit dem Ziel gestaltet, Harmonie und Gleichgewicht zu schaffen. Dieser Tradition zufolge soll die Lebensenergie, Chi genannt, harmonisch durch alle Räume des Hauses fließen.

l'espace et ce qu'il contient (même la salle de bains) afin de créer harmonie et équilibre. Selon cette tradition, l'énergie vitale, le Chi, doit se déplacer harmonieusement dans toutes les pièces. Elle peut pourtant s'échapper facilement de la salle de bains qui doit, à cause des tuyaux d'écoulement et des appareils sanitaires ouverts, rester autant que possible fermée. La salle de bains peut être revalorisée avec des couleurs et des objets au goût du propriétaire. Un autre art oriental répandu en occident est le Vastu Vidya. Cette science hindoue attire la santé et la prospérité au sein du foyer. Selon cette tradition, la salle de bains, qui est sous l'influence de la lune, est un endroit de propreté et de jovance. De ce fait elle doit toujours être très propre et embellie avec des fleurs, des plantes et des senteurs rafraîchissantes. La salle de bains, selon le Vastu, nécessite des surfaces réfléchissantes telles que des miroirs, qui doivent être posés sur les parois

ban vestidores, cuartos infantiles e incluso tocadores. De la cultura oriental recuperamos tradiciones milenarias como el feng shui, la antigua sabiduría de la China de la ubicación, que redistribuye el espacio de la vivienda (incluido el baño) para crear armonía y equilibrio. Según esta tradición, la energía vital o chi, que debe fluir armoniosamente por todas las habitaciones, puede escaparse fácilmente en el cuarto de baño, al ser la zona donde se concentran los desagües y los sanitarios abiertos, por

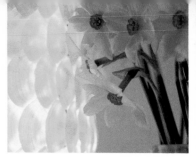

possible. In addition, the bathroom should be enhanced with objects and colors to the taste of the owner. Another oriental art that has reached the West is the Vastu Vidya. This Hindu "science" brings health and prosperity to the home. According to this tradition, the moon governs bathing. The bathroom is a place of cleanliness and rejuvenation and must therefore always be clean and replete with flowers, plants and refreshing aromas. According to Vastu, bathrooms require reflective surfaces such as mirrors hung from the north and east walls. As much as possible, the toilet should be distanced as far as possible from doors and windows, so as to guarantee intimacy. The wisdom of these traditions, increasingly influential in western society, form part of a new culture of the home—a culture which stands for the beneficial use of resources and a natural philosophy of life.

Angesichts der Tatsache, dass sich im Badezimmer viele Abflüsse und offene sanitäre Einrichtungen befinden, kann diese Lebensenergie in diesem Bereich leicht entweichen und es ist darum unbedingt notwendig, diesen Raum so geschlossen wie möglich zu halten. In Ergänzung dazu sollte das Bad durch Objekte und Farben je nach Geschmack des Besitzers verschönert werden. Eine andere asiatische Kunst, die im Westen Fuß gefasst hat, ist das Vastu Vidya, die hinduistische „Lehre" davon, wie man dem Heim zu Gesundheit und Wohlstand verhilft. Dieser Tradition zufolge wird das Bad durch den Mond regiert und ist ein Ort der Sauberkeit und Verjüngung, weshalb es immer sehr sauber und reich mit Blumen, Pflanzen und erfrischenden Düften ausgestattet sein sollte. Dem Vastu folgend ist es erforderlich, dass reflektierende Oberflächen wie Spiegel an den Nord- und Ostseiten des Bades angebracht werden. Soweit möglich, sollte die Toilette von Türen und Fenstern entfernt angebracht werden, um eine größere Intimität zu garantieren. Die Ratschläge dieser Traditionen, die sich in den westlichen Gesellschaften immer mehr verbreiten, sind ein Teil der neuen Wohnkultur, die für eine optimale Nutzung der verfügbaren Mittel und die Philosophie von einem natürlichen Leben steht.

lo que, en la medida de lo posible, deben estar siempre cerrados. El baño, además, debe realzarse con objetos y colores del gusto del propietario. Otro arte oriental extendido en occidente es el Vastu Vidya hindú, la ciencia que atrae la salud y prosperidad al hogar. Según esta tradición, el baño está regido por la luna y es lugar de limpieza y rejuvenecimiento, por lo que debe estar siempre muy limpio y repleto de flores, plantas y aromas refrescantes. El baño, según el Vastu, requiere superficies reflectantes como los espejos, colocados en las paredes norte y este. El inodoro, a ser posible, debe estar alejado de puertas y ventanas para asegurar mayor intimidad. Los consejos de estas tradiciones, cada vez más extendidas en las sociedades occidentales, forman parte de la nueva cultura de la vivienda, que defiende el aprovechamiento de recursos y una filosofía de vida natural.

Nord et Est. Les toilettes doivent si possible être éloignés des fenêtres et des portes pour assurer une intimité plus grande. Les conseils de ces traditions trouvant toujours plus d'adeptes dans le monde occidental, font partie de la nouvelle culture de l'habitation, qui préconise l'exploitation des ressources disponibles et une philosophie de vie naturelle.

ASPECTS

Aspects
du design
Aspekte
des Designs
OF DESIGN
Aspectos
de diseño

BATHROOM LAYOUT

Alongside the kitchen, the bathroom is the room in the house which requires the most planning. This is due to the fact that, once pipes and drainage have been installed redistribution of the space becomes increasingly difficult. For this reason, professional designers believe that, prior to construction, a detailed analysis of the characteristics of the available space and a priori study of the most practical features of the layout are essential. Placement of doors and drains, ventilation, as well as how to best take advantage of the available light, must be carefully considered before initiating the construction phase of the project. The bathroom is also a room intended, as much as possible, for personalized use. A rational layout must then take the priorities of the user into account. For example, it is important to know how often the bathtub will be utilized, how much storage space is needed, and how frequently the boudoir will be used. Also important to know are the desired characteristics of the fittings and selected furniture; whether, in addition to the lavatory, a bidet is to be installed; the preferred type of heating; and, finally, the required points of illumination.

Despite the fact that today's bathroom is considered a space open to the entire family, it is still a room that demands a high degree of intimacy. Its layout thus establishes divisions which allow for simultaneous use of distinct areas. The three basic zones of the bathroom are the boudoir (sink, closets and furniture piece for storing towels and other bathroom equipment), the bath-shower area (shower, bathtub, or both implements in one), and the sanitary installation area (toilet and bidet). Unless a complete renovation is desired, this final division should be situated close to the drainpipes so as to avoid adding unnecessary cost and complexity to the project. Doors and semi-partitions, the latter being very useful for lavatories, help to articulate the different parts. A partition can be used for the shower or bath. Another alternative is coming up with a differentiated layout in which each zone is independent.

The availability of space determines the character of the distribution. There are, however, tricks designed to help take maximum advantage of bathroom space. If the room is small, for example, it is better to install a shower instead of a bathtub, to do without a bidet, and to have a suspended toilet. A small built-in sink is less voluminous than one with a pedestal. The selection of light materials, simplicity of line and an ordered layout will contribute to the visual amplification of the space.

BADAUFTEILUNG

Das Badezimmer ist neben der Küche der Raum, welcher am meisten Planung erfordert, da nach dem Installieren der Leitungen und Abflussrohre eine Neuaufteilung sehr schwierig ist. Deshalb halten Fachleute es für notwendig, vor dem Beginn der Arbeiten die Eigenschaften des verfügbaren Platzes ganz genau und bis ins Detail zu analysieren und die praktischen Aspekte der Aufteilungsmöglichkeiten zu studieren: wo befindet sich der Eingang, wie ist die Lage der Abwasserleitungen, wie kann man das vorhandene Licht am besten nutzen, über welche Lüftung verfügt man. Beim Badezimmer handelt es sich um einen Raum, der an die individuellen Ansprüche des Benutzers bestmöglichst angepasst werden sollte, weshalb bei einer rationalen Aufteilung stets die Prioritäten des einzelnen Benutzers in Betracht gezogen werden müssen. Wichtig ist es zu analysieren, ob oft gebadet wird, ob viel Aufbewahrungsraum oder Lagerplatz benötigt wird, ja selbst wie häufig der Toilettentisch benutzt werden wird und welche Eigenschaften die ausgewählten sanitären Anlagen und Möbel haben, ob nur ein WC oder auch ein Bidet zu installieren ist, welches Heizungssystem bevorzugt wird und welche Beleuchtungspunkte im Badezimmer benötigt werden.

Obwohl das Badezimmer heutzutage als offener Raum begriffen wird, der der ganzen Familie und auch mehreren Familienmitgliedern zur selben Zeit zur Verfügung steht, verlangt er doch immer noch einen hohen Grad an Intimität für den Einzelnen. Das ist einer der Gründe, warum die Raumaufteilung Trennungen zwischen den Funktionsbereichen vorsehen sollte, welche die gleichzeitige Benutzung durch mehrere Personen möglich machen. Die drei grundlegenden Bereiche des Badezimmers sind der Toilettentisch (inklusive des Waschbeckens und der Badezimmerschränke, in welchen man die Hygieneartikel sowie die Hand- und Badetücher unterbringt), die Nasszone (inklusive Dusche und Badewanne, beziehungsweise der kombinierten Lösung aus diesen beiden Elementen) und der Sanitärbereich (in welchem das Bidet und das WC installiert werden). Der zuletzt genannte Bereich sollte in der Nähe des Abflussrohres liegen, da sonst eine umfassende Sanierung benötigt werden würde, die erheblich umfangreichere und kostenspieligere Arbeiten zur Folge haben würde. Die verschiedenen Zonen können durch Türen, halbhohe Mauern (besonders im Sanitärbereich eine angemessene Lösung), Trennwände (für Dusche und Badewanne) oder einfach durch eine klar differenzierte Aufteilung als unabhängige Bereiche gekennzeichnet werden.

Abhängig ist diese Aufteilung vom verfügbaren Platz. Es existieren allerdings ein paar Kniffe, die für die optimale Ausnützung des vorhandenen Raumes hilfreich sein können.

Bei kleinen Räumen ist die Installation einer Dusche der einer Badewanne vorzuziehen, genauso wie es hier sinnvoll ist, auf das Bidet zu verzichten und ein Wand-WC zu wählen. Ein kleines, eingebautes Waschbecken ist weniger voluminös als eine Waschgelegenheit mit Fuß oder Sockel. Die Auswahl von leichten Materialien, Einfachheit in der Linienführung und eine geordnete Gliederung lassen den Raum ebenfalls optisch größer erscheinen.

CONCEPTION DE LA SALLE DE BAINS

A côté de la cuisine, la salle de bains est la pièce de la maison qui nécessite une planification soigneuse. Cela est dû au fait qu'une fois que les conduites d'eau et les lignes électriques sont installées il est pratiquement impossible de changer les éléments de place. Les spécialistes croient qu'il est indispensable d'analyser en détail les caractéristiques des lieux et d'étudier les aspects pratiques de la répartition: Où se trouve la porte d'accès et les tuyaux d'écoulement, comment utiliser au mieux l'éclairage existant et l'aération disponible ... Il s'agit d'une pièce devant s'adapter au mieux aux besoins personnels de son utilisateur. C'est pour cela qu'une répartition rationnelle doit tenir compte des priorités du propriétaire. Il est important d'analyser si on se baigne souvent, si on a besoin de beaucoup de place de rangement, si la table de toilette est employée fréquemment, quelles sont les caractéristiques des divers sanitaires et meubles choisis, si on désire uniquement des toilettes ou également un bidet, quel est le mode de chauffage désiré et de quel éclairage aurons nous besoin dans la salle de bains.

Cette pièce demande une grande intimité bien qu'elle soit conçue actuellement comme un lieu ouvert à toute la famille. Une répartition comportant des divisions permet d'utiliser les différentes parties simultanément. Les trois zones principales sont la table de toilette (lavabo, et armoires permettant de ranger les serviettes et les divers ustensiles de la salle de bains), la zone de l'eau (avec la douche, la baignoire, ou les deux ensembles) et la zone des sanitaires (où sont installés les toilettes et le bidet), cette dernière étant placée à proximité des tuyaux d'écoulement à moins que l'on décide de transformer le tout ce qui est généralement très cher et très compliqué. Les différentes parties étant séparées par des portes ou des petits murs (important en particulier pour les toilettes), des cloisons (pour la douche et la baignoire), ou simplement de par une répartition clairement différenciée rendant chacune des zones indépendantes.

La répartition se fait en fonction de l'espace disponible. Il existe quelques-uns trucs pour en tirer le meilleur parti. Si la pièce est petite il est mieux d'installer une douche au lieu d'une baignoire, de renoncer à un bidet et d'opter pour des toilettes suspendues. Un petit lavabo encastré est moins volumineux qu'un lavabo à pied. Le choix de matériaux légers, la simplicité des lignes et une répartition ordonnée contribuent à agrandir optiquement l'espace.

DISTRIBUCIÓN DEL BAÑO

El cuarto de baño es, junto a la cocina, la estancia que requiere más planificación de toda la casa, puesto que una vez instaladas todas las tuberías y bajantes es muy difícil volver a redistribuir el espacio. Por este motivo los profesionales creen imprescindible, antes de iniciar una obra, analizar con detalle las características del espacio disponible y estudiar a priori los aspectos más prácticos de la distribución: dónde se sitúa la puerta de acceso, cuál es la situación de los desagües, cómo aprovechar la luz existente, de qué ventilación se dispone. Se trata de una habitación que ha de adaptarse al máximo al uso personalizado del usuario, por lo que una distribución racional debe estudiar las prioridades de su propietario. Es importante analizar si se va a tomar un baño a menudo, si se necesita mucho espacio de almacenamiento, si va a utilizarse mucho el tocador, qué características tienen los sanitarios y los muebles elegidos, si se va a colocar sólo el inodoro o también el bidé, qué tipo de calefacción se prefiere y qué puntos de iluminación necesitará el cuarto de baño.

Esta habitación requiere un alto grado de intimidad, aunque actualmente se conciba como un espacio abierto a toda la familia. De ahí que su distribución establezca divisiones para que puedan ser usadas simultáneamente. Las tres zonas básicas del baño son el tocador (con el lavamanos, armarios y el mueble para almacenar toallas y enseres de baño), la zona de aguas (con la ducha, la bañera o los dos elementos a la vez) y la zona de los sanitarios (donde se instalan el inodoro y el bidé). Esta última división debe situarse cerca del bajante de aguas, a menos que se quiera iniciar una reforma completa, lo que haría el proceso mucho más caro y complicado. Las diferentes partes pueden señalarse mediante puertas o muretes (muy adecuado para los sanitarios), con una mampara (para la ducha o la bañera) o simplemente proyectando una distribución claramente diferenciada, de forma que cada zona sea independiente.

La distribución se establece en función del espacio disponible. Existen algunos trucos que pueden ayudar a aprovechar los metros del baño. Si la estancia es pequeña, es mejor instalar una ducha y no una bañera, prescindir del bidé y utilizar un inodoro suspendido. Un pequeño lavamanos encastrado es menos voluminoso que uno con pedestal. La elección de materiales ligeros, la simplicidad de líneas y una distribución ordenada contribuirán a ampliar visualmente el espacio.

FURNITURE

Essential to the bathroom is its furniture. This is because furniture solves the problem of storage in a room where order and hygiene are of paramount importance. Bathroom furniture tends to be situated in the boudoir. Nevertheless, secondary pieces placed next to the lavatory to store hygienic paper and shelves or niches in the bath-shower area allowing for the ready availability of sponges and soap are also practical solutions. Bathroom closets or auxiliary pieces require special treatment in order to withstand exposure to water and humidity. Models made of resistant materials like treated wood or lacquered surfaces or light structures made of glass should be chosen. Normally, the bathroom tends to be a room of slight dimension. However, there exist many designs and solutions with large capacity to store the gamut of bathroom equipment: towels, cosmetic products, soaps, and accessories. If a bathroom requires large storage space, the best option is to install built-in closets with sliding doors or blinds. Furniture pieces that fit below the sink allow for advantage to be taken of the void created by this fitting. In some instances, this type of furniture has a covering of the same material as the sink. Another solution is to install a projecting shelf, which adds lightness to the space. In the cases where there is not sufficient space to locate auxiliary furniture, niches can be built into the walls. Another good way to optimize space consists in installing shelves or small furniture pieces in the wall. Carts or auxiliary pieces with wheels are practical solutions whose portability permits easy access to bathroom equipment. In bathrooms of very limited size, small shelves to hold soap baskets and cologne are effective. Installing a towel rail is another means of optimizing every last bit of space. Wether of wood, glass, steel or aluminium, these modules are the best means of assuring that the bathroom is always in order. On the market are multitudinous designs conceived for all sorts of bathrooms: rustic models with wrought iron furniture and wickerwork; wood structures recalling classical spaces; or steel modules suited for more contemporary environments.

MÖBLIERUNG

Auch das Badezimmer kommt ohne den Einsatz von Einzelmöbeln nicht aus. Sie lösen in diesem Raum, der in besonderer Weise Ordnung und Hygiene erfordert, das Problem der Aufbewahrung. In diesem Raum werden Möbel bevorzugt in der Nähe des Toilettentisches, neben dem Waschbecken, platziert, da dies der Ort ist, an dem die meisten Accessoires verwendet werden. Doch auch in der Nähe des Sanitärbereichs sind Hilfsmöbel praktisch (zum Beispiel zur Lagerung von Toilettenpapier) genauso wie Regale und Mauernischen in der Nasszone von Vorteil sind (zur Ablage von Seifen und Schwämmen). Schränke und sonstige Zusatzmöbel des Badezimmers benötigen eine spezielle Oberflächenbehandlung, damit sie der Einwirkung von Wasser und Feuchtigkeit standhalten können. Dementsprechend sollten widerstandsfähige Modelle gewählt werden, die aus behandeltem Holz oder leichten Materialien wie Glas bestehen oder lackierte Oberflächen aufweisen. Normalerweise ist das Badezimmer ein kleiner Raum. Es gibt jedoch zahlreiche Entwürfe für Badezimmermöbel mit viel Stauraum, in denen alle Gerätschaften des Bades wie Handtücher, kosmetische Produkte, Seifen und sonstige Utensilien untergebracht werden können und die auch in kleinen Bädern Platz finden. Bei Bädern, in welchen viel Stauraum benötigt wird, sind Einbauschränke mit Schiebetüren oder Jalousien besonders praktisch. Ein Möbelstück unter der Waschgelegenheit ist eine weitere gelungene Lösung, da sie den Hohlraum unter dem Waschbecken ausnützt. In einigen Fällen ist bei diesem Möbelstück eine Arbeits- und Abstellfläche aus dem gleichen Material vorzufinden. Eine andere Möglichkeit ist das Anbringen eines Hängeregals, welches dem Raum eine gewisse Leichtigkeit gibt, sowie der Einbau von Mauernischen an Wänden, eine Lösung für Badezimmer, die nicht über den notwendigen Platz für Zusatzmöbel verfügen. Auch Wandregale oder kleinere, an der Wand hängende Möbel nutzen den Raum optimal aus. Verschiebbare Wägelchen oder andere Hilfsmöbel auf Rollen, machen es möglich, alles jederzeit und an jedem Ort des Bades zur Hand zu haben. Besonders kleine Bäder können auch mit Hilfe von Eckregalen für Seife, Parfüm oder Handtüchern bis in die letzte Ecke ausgenutzt werden. All diese Kleinmöbel, gleichgültig ob sie aus Glas, Stahl oder Aluminium hergestellt wurden, sind die besten Verbündeten im Kampf gegen die Unordnung im Bad. Sie werden in verschiedenen Designs, für die unterschiedlichsten Stilrichtungen hergestellt: rustikale Modelle mit Möbeln aus Schmiedeeisenteilen und Korb, Holzstrukturen, die dem Raum eine klassische Note geben oder auch Stahlmodule für ein modernes Ambiente.

LE MOBILIER

Le mobilier est indispensable dans la salle de bains permettant de résoudre les problèmes de rangement dans une pièce où l'ordre et l'hygiène ont une grande importance. Les meubles sont placés à proximité de la table de toilette, à côté du lavabo du fait que c'est l'endroit où l'on emploie la majorité des articles de toilette. Ils peuvent également être placés à côté des sanitaires (pour ranger les rouleaux de papier WC). Les niches et les étagères présentent un avantage dans la zone « eau » (pour avoir constamment savon et éponge à portée de main). Les armoires et les meubles auxiliaires de la salles de bains nécessitent un traitement particulier leur permettant de supporter l'eau et l'humidité. On doit choisir des modèles réalisés avec des matériaux résistants tels que le bois traité, les surfaces vernies ou de structure légère comme le verre. En général la salle de bain est une pièce de petite taille. Il existe de multiples designs et possibilités ayant de grande capacité pour ranger ce dont on a besoin dans la salle de bains comme les serviettes de bain, les produits cosmétiques, les savons et divers accessoires. Si une salle de bain nécessite beaucoup de place de rangement, la meilleure solution est d'installer des armoires encastrables avec des portes coulissantes ou à persiennes. Les meubles placés sous le lavabo permettent d'exploiter au mieux cet espace libre. Certain d'entre eux ont un pourtour du même matériel. Une autre solution étant de suspendre une étagère, ce qui ajoutent une certaine légèreté à l'endroit ou de construire une niche dans l'une des parois, surtout si on n'a pas suffisamment de place pour y mettre des meubles auxiliaires. Une bonne solution pour exploiter l'espace au maximum est de suspendre des armoires ou des étagères à la parois. Les chariots et les meubles auxiliaires sur roues sont pratiques et permettent d'avoir ce dont on a besoin à portée de main. Dans les petites salles de bains on peut fixer des petites étagères dans les coins avec de petites corbeilles à savons et des bouteilles de parfum, ainsi que des porte-serviettes. Ces éléments sont les meilleurs alliés pour avoir toujours de l'ordre dans la salle de bains. Elles peuvent être en bois, en verre en acier ou en aluminium. Il existe sur le marché de multiples designs pouvant s'adapter à tous les styles de salle de bains. Des modèles rustiques avec un mobilier en fer forgé et en osier, en bois de structure classique ou en acier pour une ambiance plus moderne.

71

MOBILIARIO

El mobiliario es un elemento imprescindible en el cuarto de baño, puesto que soluciona el problema del almacenamiento en una estancia que precisa orden e higiene. Los muebles tienden a situarse en la zona de tocador, junto al lavabo, puesto que es el lugar donde se emplean la mayoría de los complementos, aunque también resultan prácticos los muebles auxiliares cerca de los sanitarios (para almacenar el papel higiénico) y las baldas u hornacinas en la zona de aguas (para tener siempre a mano esponjas y jabones). Los armarios o muebles auxiliares de baño requieren un tratamiento especial que soporte el agua y la humedad, por lo que deben elegirse modelos fabricados con materiales resistentes como la madera tratada, las superficies lacadas o las estructuras ligeras como el cristal. Por norma general, el baño tiende a ser una habitación de reducidas dimensiones. Existen múltiples diseños y soluciones de gran capacidad que se adaptan a espacios mínimos para almacenar todos los enseres del baño como toallas, productos cosméticos, jabones y accesorios. Si el baño requiere de un gran espacio de almacenamiento, la mejor opción es instalar armarios empotrados con puertas correderas o persianas. Los muebles bajolavabo son otra buena opción, muy utilizada para aprovechar el hueco del lavamanos. En algunos casos, este tipo de muebles incorpora una encimera del mismo material. Otra solución es instalar un estante volado, que añade ligereza, aunque también puede construirse una hornacina en una de las paredes, sobre todo si no hay suficientes metros para colocar muebles auxiliares. Una buena forma de aprovechar el espacio consiste en instalar estanterías o pequeños muebles en la pared. Los carritos o muebles auxiliares con ruedas son una solución práctica que permite tenerlo todo a mano, y pueden ser desplazados de un lado al otro. En los baños de poca superficie pueden aprovecharse todos los rincones para instalar pequeños estantes, con cestos con jabones y botes de colonia, o bien instalar un toallero. De madera, cristal, acero o aluminio, estos módulos son los mejores aliados para conseguir que el baño esté siempre en orden. En el mercado existen múltiples diseños pensados para adaptarse a todos los estilos del baño: modelos rústicos, con mobiliario de hierro de forja y mimbre, estructuras de madera que pueden recrean espacios clásicos o módulos de acero para ambientes más actuales.

MATERIALS AND COVERINGS

The materials utilized for bathroom coverings must be highly resistant while at the same time practical and aesthetically pleasing. Today, professional designers shuffle between various combinations in the creation of original and functional spaces. Wood is a natural material that adds warmth to any space and a common used bathroom material as for example for furniture pieces. Tropical wood is the most adequate kind for the bath-shower area. Iroko, teak, bolondo, merbau, and wengue are the most utilized types of wood, given that their high oil content makes them especially resistant to contact with water. Other types of wood such as cedar, birch, oak or cherry are also ideal for the bathroom once they have been treated. Wood also allows for the creation of distinctive decorative environments: rustic, classical, and more modern. Its different tones can give rise to luminous spaces or more sophisticated ones. Marble is a very useful covering for creating elegant environments, and is thus a highly valued bathroom material. Resistant to humidity, its main drawback is its frigid appearance. Intelligently combined with warmer materials, however, marble contributes to the creation of a distinguished and functional space. Tile is an effective solution for all sorts of environments. It is a material very well suited for covering walls and, given the fact that tile is impermeable, ideal for bathrooms. There is an infinite range of sizes and colors, as well as sophisticated designs that imitate more delicate textures. Another often utilized option is mosaic. These small ceramic or glass tiles are ideal for areas where contact with water is high. Though manufactured in various sizes, the most widespread mosaic tile measurement is the miniscule 1.5 x 1.5 cm. Paint with special humidity-resistant finish is an option whose outcome is highly decorative. Yet, as with painted vinyl paper, this alternative is best suited for the boudoir. New designs experiment with other materials, such as cement, natural stones, plastic coverings and laminated metal. As a rule, they are highly resistant and produce spectacular effects.

MATERIALIEN UND VERKLEIDUNGEN

Die Verkleidungsmaterialien des Badezimmers sollen nicht nur praktisch und dekorativ sein, sie müssen auch eine sehr hohe Widerstandsfähigkeit aufweisen. Heutzutage mischen die professionellen Designer verschiedene Stilrichtungen und kreieren so sowohl funktionale als auch originelle Räume. Holz ist ein natürliches Material, das in der Lage ist, jedem Raum eine warme Ausstrahlung zu verleihen. Es gehört zu den häufig im Badezimmer verwendeten Werkstoffen, und wird besonders für Badezimmermöbel eingesetzt. Tropenhölzer sind für den Nassbereich am besten geeignet. Iroco, Bolondo, Merbau, Wengue und Teakholz werden hier bevorzugt eingesetzt, da diese durch ihren hohen Fettgehalt gegen Wassereinwirkung am unempfindlichsten sind. Aber auch andere Holzarten, wie Kirschbaum, Eiche, Buche oder Zeder sind gut verwendbar, sofern sie einer speziellen Oberflächenbehandlung unterzogen werden. Durch Holz lassen sich verschiedene Stilrichtungen kreieren: rustikale, klassische, moderne. Da es in unterschiedlichen Farbtönen erhältlich ist, kann es dem Raum sowohl einen sehr hellen als auch einen anspruchsvollen Charakter verleihen. Marmor ist eine Verkleidung, die prädestiniert für ein elegantes Ambiente ist und die daher bei der Ausstattung des Bades bevorzugt eingesetzt wird. Sehr resistent gegen Feuchtigkeit, ist ein generelles Problem bei der Verwendung dieses Materials jedoch sein kaltes Erscheinungsbild, dem man aber durch die Kombination mit wärmeren Materialien entgegenwirken kann. Auf diese Weise ist es möglich, einen Raum zu schaffen, der ein gehobenes Ambiente mit Funktionalität verbindet. Der Einsatz von Fliesen bietet die Möglichkeit, jede Stilrichtung zu verwirklichen. Sie sind besonders als Verkleidung von Wänden, und auf Grund ihrer hohen Widerstandsfähigkeit und Wasserresistenz optimal für den Einsatz im Badezimmer geeignet. Fliesen sind in einer nahezu unendlichen Vielfalt von Formaten, Größen und Farben, ja selbst in raffinierten Designs erhältlich, die empfindlichere Materialien nachahmen. Auch Mosaikkacheln werden gerne im Bad eingesetzt. Sie bestehen aus einer Vielzahl von kleinen Teilchen aus Keramik oder Glas, die optimal für Bereiche sind, die oft mit Wasser in Berührung kommen. Die am weitest verbreiteten Mosaikkacheln haben eine Größe von 1,5 x 1,5 cm, werden jedoch auch in anderen Größen hergestellt. Spezielle Farbanstriche stellen, genau wie Vinyltapeten, eine sehr dekorative Möglichkeit der Wandverkleidung dar. Sie werden am sinnvollsten im Bereich des Toilettentisches eingesetzt. Moderne Designs experimentieren heute auch mit anderen Materialien, wie Zement, Naturstein, Plastikverkleidungen und Metalllaminaten. In der Regel sind diese neuen Materialien sehr widerstandsfähig und erzeugen spektakuläre Effekte.

MATÉRIAUX ET REVÊTEMENTS

Les matériaux de revêtement employés dans la salle de bains doivent être très résistants, de même que pratiques et décoratifs. Les spécialistes tiennent tout une palette de combinaisons fonctionnelles et originales à notre disposition. Le bois est un élément conférant à chaque espace beaucoup de chaleur. Il s'agit d'un des matériaux les plus employés dans la salle de bains spécialement pour le mobilier. Les bois tropicaux sont les plus adéquats pour la zone de l'eau : l'iroco, le teck, le bolondo, le merbeau et le wengué sont les plus courants, leur haut contenu en huiles les rend particulièrement résistants à l'eau. D'autres bois tels le cèdre, le hêtre, le chêne et le cerisier conviennent une fois traitées, parfaitement à cette pièce. Le bois permet de créer des ambiances décoratives très distinctes: rustiques, classiques ou plus actuelles. Les différentes tonalités permettent de créer des espaces lumineux ou plus sophistiqués. Le marbre est un revêtement très approprié. Il est très apprécié dans la salle de bains car il lui donne beaucoup d'élégance. Il est résistant à l'humidité son principal désavantage étant son aspect froid qu'on peut facilement éviter en le combinant avec des éléments plus chauds. Le carrelage constitue une bonne solution pour tous les types d'ambiances. Résistant et n'étant pas poreux, il est idéal pour revêtir les parois de la salle de bains. Il en existe un choix infini de toutes les tailles, de toutes les couleurs et de design très sophistiqués imitant des textures plus délicates. Une autre option très appréciée et la mosaïque. Ces petits carreaux de céramique ou de verre sont parfaits pour une pièce humide. On les trouve de plusieurs tailles mais les plus courantes sont de 1,5 x 1,5 cm. Une peinture spéciale résistante à l'eau s'avère être une option très décorative de même que le papier peint en vinyle pour les parois aux alentours de la table de toilette. Aujourd'hui on expérimente avec d'autres matériaux comme le ciment, les pierres naturelles, les revêtements en plastique ou en métal laminé. Ces nouveaux matériaux sont en général très résistant et produisent des effets spectaculaires.

MATERIALES Y REVESTIMIENTOS

Los materiales que han de revestir el cuarto de baño deben ser muy resistentes, a la vez que prácticos y decorativos. En la actualidad los profesionales estudian múltiples combinaciones para crear espacios originales y funcionales. La madera es un elemento natural que añade calidez a cualquier espacio. Se utiliza frecuentemente en el baño, además de en el mobiliario. La madera tropical es la más adecuada en la zona de aguas: el iroco, junto con la teca, el bolondo, el merbau y el wengué son los tipos más utilizados, puesto que su alto contenido en grasa las hace especialmente resistentes al contacto con el agua. Otros tipos de madera como el cedro, el haya, el roble o el cerezo resultan también óptimas para esta estancia una vez ha sido tratada. La madera permite crear distintos ambientes decorativos: rústicos, clásicos, actuales y las distintas tonalidades consiguen espacios luminosos o lugares más sofisticados. El mármol es un revestimiento muy apropiado para crear ambientes elegantes, por lo que constituye un material muy apreciado en el baño. Resistente a la humedad, su principal problema es el frío aspecto que presenta, aunque si se combina bien con materiales más cálidos puede lograr un espacio distinguido y muy funcional. Los azulejos constituyen una buena solución para todo tipo de ambientes. Son muy adecuados para revestir todas las paredes y, al no ser un material poroso, resisten muy bien en los cuartos de baño. Existen infinidad de gamas, medidas y colores e incluso diseños más sofisticados, que imitan texturas más delicadas. Otra opción muy utilizada es el gresite. Se trata de pequeñas teselas de cerámica o de vidrio, ideales para la zona donde el contacto con el agua es mayor. La medida más extendida son la minúsculas piezas de 1,5 x 1,5 cm, aunque se fabrican en varios tamaños. La pintura con acabados especiales que soporta la humedad puede resultar una opción muy decorativa, aunque, igual que el papel vinílico pintado, es mejor situarla en la zona del tocador. Los nuevos diseños se atreven con otros materiales como el cemento, la piedra natural, los revestimientos plásticos y las láminas metálicas. Por norma general, los nuevos materiales son muy resistentes y producen efectos espectaculares.

BATHROOM COLOR

The first step in defining the style of a room is selecting the color of walls and coverings. While election of color and coverings is one of the most subjective factors of the decoration, the visual effects produced by different tones on walls and furniture are well known. Color is used to decorate an environment, but it can also partly solve spatial problems given that some colors visually amplify a room. Different colors react differently to natural light. Red tones (e.g., orange or yellow) are considered warm tones. By intensifying the reflection of natural light, they create intense environments. Tones closer to blue and violet are cool tones that distance walls and diffuse light so that the space seems clearer. Along with the entire range of yellow, white expands and intensifies the clarity of the space, producing brilliant effects and adding more light to the room. Clear and luminous colors give rise to a visual effect which makes the space seem larger. As such, these colors are especially suitable for small bathrooms. On the other hand, darker colors seem to diminish bathroom size and are thus effective in large spaces that require more intimacy or seek originality and contrast. In another sense, colors also influence mood. Cool colors transmit a sensation of tranquility and thus facilitate rest and relaxation, making them a good choice for more intimate areas such as bathrooms and bedrooms. Neutral tones such as white and natural colors, as well as pastels blended with a large amount of white, communicate a sensation of hygiene and immaculateness, and, therefore, are also considered adequate for bathrooms. More intense colors transmit a sensation of vitality. In theory they are not recommended for rooms where tranquility is the goal. That much said there is no fixed rule prohibiting multiple combinations or use of warmer colors in bathrooms. The subtle differences in tones that can be produced are enormous. A color that is considered warm can be diluted to the point where it converts into a pastel tone. As the decoration seeks to create a space to the liking of the person who will use it, it is better to choose colors on a subjective basis. Many combinations can be made. If more prominence for furniture and fittings is desired, a neutral background is the best choice.

DIE FARBAUSWAHL IM BADEZIMMER

Die Wahl der Wandfarbe und der Verkleidungen ist der erste Schritt zur Bestimmung der Stilrichtung, die ein Zimmer erhalten soll. Dieser Aspekt der Dekoration wird zwar am subjektivsten empfunden, aber der visuelle Effekt, den der Farbton der Wand oder der Möbel hat, ist allgemein bekannt. Farbe kann teilweise auch Platzprobleme lösen, da einige Farben den Raum optisch größer erscheinen lassen: Unterschiedliche Farben reagieren unterschiedlich auf natürliches Licht. Rotstichige Farben, wie Gelb oder Orange, werden als warme Töne angesehen, sie verstärken die Reflektion des natürlichen Lichtes, und können auf diese Weise eine starke Atmosphäre erzeugen. Farben, die eher dem Blau oder Violett nahe stehen, sind kältere Töne, die die Wände eines Raumes entfernter erscheinen und das Licht vor dem menschlichen Auge verschwimmen lassen, sodass der Raum selbst klarer hervortritt. Weiß verstärkt die Klarheit eines Raumes, ebenso wie die Palette der gelben Farbtöne, die brillante Effekte erzeugt und die Wirkung des Lichtes in einem Raum verstärkt. Helle und leuchtende Farben vergrößern den Raum optisch und sind dadurch besonders für kleine Bäder geeignet. Umgekehrt verkleinern dunkle Farben die Größe eines Zimmers. Sie sind daher besonders wirkungsvoll in größeren Badezimmern, für die man sich eine intimere Atmosphäre oder stärkere Kontraste und mehr Charakter wünscht. Auf der anderen Seite beeinflussen Farben auch unsere Stimmung. Kalte Farbtöne vermitteln das Gefühl von Ruhe und erleichtern so Entspannung und Erholung, weswegen sie gerade für intime Räume wie das Schlafzimmer oder das Badezimmer geeignet sind. Neutrale Farben wie Weiß, Beige und alle Pastelltöne (d. h. Farbtöne, die viel weiß enthalten) vermitteln das Gefühl von Hygiene und Sauberkeit und passen daher sehr gut zur Atmospäre eines Badezimmers. Warme, intensive Farben vermitteln das Gefühl von Vitalität. Daher werden sie normalerweise nicht für Räume empfohlen, in denen man Entspannung sucht. Trotzdem gibt es keine festen Regeln, die die Verwendung verschiedenartiger Farbkombinationen verbieten oder einen daran hindern würden, wärmere Töne für das Badezimmer zu wählen. Farbtöne können heute in feinsten Abstufungen hergestellt werden, und sogar eine Farbe, die eher als warm angesehen wird, kann durch Abschwächung in einen Pastellton verwandelt werden. Da das Ziel einer Dekoration in erster Linie darin besteht, einen Raum nach dem Geschmack und den Bedürfnissen des Benutzers zu entwerfen, fährt man am besten damit, die Farben nach dessen subjektiven Empfinden auszuwählen. Eine Vielzahl an Kombinationen ist möglich und soll der Effekt erreicht werden, das Mobiliar und die sanitären Einrichtungen in den Vordergrund zu stellen, sollte der Farbhintergrund eher neutral gehalten sein.

LE COULEUR DES SALLES DE BAINS

Le choix de la couleur et du revêtement des parois est le premier pas pour définir le style d'une pièce. Bien qu'il s'agisse de l'un des facteurs le plus subjectif de la décoration, il est bien connu que chaque ton de la paroi et du mobilier a un effet optique. La couleur est utilisée pour décorer l'environnement et peut partiellement du moins résoudre des problèmes d'espace du fait que certaines couleurs amplifient visuellement une pièce. Les couleurs ressortent différemment à la lumière naturelle créant une impression chaleureuse. Les tons tirant sur le rouge, comme l'orange et le jaune sont considérés comme chaud et intensifient la réflexion de la lumière. Les tons allant vers le bleu et le violet sont froid et mettent une distance entre les parois diffusant une lumière qui semble éclaircir l'espace. Le blanc agrandi et intensifie la clarté d'un espace de même que toute la gamme des jaunes qui produisent un effet brillant et donne plus de luminosité à une pièce. Les couleurs claires et lumineuses provoquent un effet optique agrandissant et sont particulièrement indiquées pour les petites salles de bains, tandis que les couleurs foncées produisent le contraire et peuvent être utilisées pour des salles de bains de grande dimension qui recherchent à obtenir une plus grande intimité ou le contraste et l'originalité. Dans un autre sens, les couleurs influencent notre état d'âme. Les couleurs froides transmettent une sensation de tranquillité et favorisent le repos et la relaxation, ce qui représente une bonne option pour les zones plus intimes comme la salle de bains ou la chambre à coucher. Les tons neutres comme le blanc, les tons naturels et pastels (nuancés avec une grande quantité de blanc) donnent une sensation d'hygiène et de pureté et son de ce fait également recommandé pour la salle de bains. Les couleurs chaudes sont plus intenses et transmettent une sensation de vitalité et ne sont en général pas recommandé pour les endroits où l'on recherche la tranquillité. Tout cela pour dire qu'il n'existe en fin de compte pas de règle fixe empêchant de multiples combinaisons ou l'emploi de couleurs chaudes pour la salle de bains. Les différences subtiles de tons que l'on peut reproduire est énorme, même une couleur dite chaude peut-être abaissée et convertie en une teinte pastel. L'intention de la décoration étant de créer un espace agréable à ceux qui l'utilisent, le meilleur est d'opter pour les couleurs préférées de chacun. On peut faire de nombreuses combinaisons. Si on veut donner plus d'importance aux meubles et aux sanitaires, il est bon de partir d'un ton neutre.

EL COLOR DEL BAÑO

Elegir el color de paredes y revestimientos es el primer paso para definir el estilo de una estancia. Aunque se trata de uno de los factores más subjetivos de la decoración, es bien conocido el efecto visual que produce cada tono en la pared o en el mobiliario. El color se utiliza para decorar un ambiente, pero además puede solucionar problemas de espacio, puesto que algunos colores amplían visualmente una habitación: los colores inciden de forma diferente sobre la luz natural. Los tonos próximos al rojo, como el naranja o el amarillo, se consideran cálidos e intensifican los reflejos de la luz natural al crear ambientes intensos. Los tonos más cercanos al azul y al violeta son colores fríos, que alejan la pared y difuminan la luz, de modo que el espacio parece más claro. El color blanco expande e intensifica la claridad de un espacio, igual que toda la gama de amarillos, que produce efectos brillantes y añade más luminosidad a una estancia. Los colores claros y luminosos provocan un efecto visual que agranda el espacio, por lo que son especialmente indicados en los baños pequeños. Y al revés, los colores más oscuros empequeñecen el baño y pueden utilizarse en grandes espacios que requieran mayor intimidad o que busquen la originalidad y el contraste. En otro sentido, los diferentes colores influyen en nuestro estado de ánimo. Los colores fríos transmiten una sensación de tranquilidad y facilitan el descanso y la relajación, así que suponen una buena opción para las zonas más íntimas, como baños y dormitorios. Los tonos neutros como el blanco y el crudo, y los colores pastel (matizados con una gran cantidad de blanco) trasmiten sensación de higiene y pulcritud, por lo que también se consideran adecuados en el cuarto de baño. Más intensos son los colores cálidos que trasmiten sensación de vitalidad y en principio no se aconsejan en las estancias donde se busca la tranquilidad. A pesar de estas premisas, no existe ninguna regla fija que impida hacer múltiples combinaciones o utilizar colores más cálidos para un cuarto de baño. Las sutiles diferencias de tonos que pueden producirse son enormes; un color que se considera cálido puede rebajarse hasta convertirse en un tono pastel. Puesto que la finalidad de la decoración consiste en proyectar un espacio agradable para quien lo utilice, lo mejor es optar por los colores preferidos de cada uno. Pueden hacerse múltiples combinaciones y, si lo que se quiere es dar mayor protagonismo al mobiliario y a los sanitarios, es mejor partir de un fondo neutro.

BATHROOM ILLUMINATION

Without a doubt the best bathroom light is natural light. This is because natural light does not distort colors and makes precision tasks such as applying makeup or shaving much easier. Bathrooms with windows should avoid curtains, roller blinds, or overly opaque glass that block exterior light. Fine cloths and translucent glass allow for maintenance of intimacy without being obstacles to the passage of light. Even with very luminous spaces, attention must be given to placement of artificial illumination to be used when the sun goes down. Bathrooms require a warm uniform kind of artificial light. Installing various halogen lights along the ceiling is, therefore, an effective alternative. This type of illumination produces a white light very similar to natural light. In addition to general illumination of the space, the dressing table demands special attention. Two light fixtures at the topmost extremes or to the sides of the mirror achieve the proper illumination, allowing for homogenous lighting of the face. Another option is lights placed in a line just above the mirror. This alternative is effective as long as light is not directly reflected in the mirror, the result of which would be unpleasantly dazzling reflections. These lights should have a vapor-resistant shade, and untreated natural materials should be avoided. These shades need be neither too opaque nor overly intense in color to avoid distortion of light. Some lights have an extendible arm. Arranged side by side, they permit changing the direction of light according to necessity. For safety purposes, hanging lamps and bulbs unprotected by shades are not recommended. Lighting the shower-bathtub area is not necessary, as the general bathroom illumination lights built into the ceiling sufficiently illuminate the zone. If desired, however, indirect light may be added in order to create a warmer, more relaxing environment. In this case, safety compartments designed to endure direct contact with water should be used. Another protective element is halogen lights with glass shades. In theory, the lavatory zone does not require its own lighting. In any case, if enhancement of a particular bathroom area is desired, fixtures directed toward this zone can be installed. Fixtures situated on glass-protected paintings, for example, give rise to a more personalized bathroom environment.

BELEUCHTUNG IM BADEZIMMER

Am günstigsten im Badezimmer ist ohne Zweifel das natürliche Licht, da es Farben nicht verfälscht und Tätigkeiten wie das Rasieren oder das Schminken, welche große Präzision erfordern, erleichtert. Daher sollte bei Bädern mit Fenstern auf Gardinen, Jalousien oder massives lichtundurchlässiges Fensterglas verzichtet werden, da sie den natürlichen Lichteinfall von außen beeinträchtigen. Dünne Stoffe und lichtdurchlässiges Glas hingegen bewahren die Intimssphäre, ohne den Lichteinfall von außen zu stören. Aber auch in sehr hellen Räumen sollte auf die Platzierung der künstlichen Beleuchtung geachtet werden, deren Benutzung nach dem Verschwinden des Tageslichts in jedem Fall notwendig ist. Im Badezimmer wird eine gleichmäßige, warme Beleuchtung benötigt. Dies wird z. B. durch verschiedene, in die Decke eingelassene Halogenlampen erreicht, die ein weißes, dem natürlichen sehr ähnliches Licht erzeugen. Zusätzlich zu dieser allgemeinen Raumbeleuchtung bedarf der Bereich des Toilettentisches besonderer Aufmerksamkeit. Zwei Wandleuchten, welche an den zwei oberen Enden des Spiegels oder an seinen Seiten installiert sind, erzeugen eine passende Beleuchtung und lassen das Gesicht des Betrachters in einem homogenen Licht erscheinen. Es ist auch möglich, die Lampen in einer Reihe über dem Spiegel anzuordnen. Allerdings sollte man hier darauf achten, dass das Licht nicht im Spiegel reflektiert wird, um blendende und störende Lichtspiegelungen zu vermeiden. Die Wandleuchten sollten mit einem Schirm ausgestattet sein, der gegen Wasserdampf resistent ist. Auf natürliche Materialien ohne zusätzliche Behandlung sollte verzichtet werden. Der Schirm sollte nicht zu wenig Licht durchlassen und seine Farbe nicht zu intensiv sein, da die Stärke des Lichteinfalls sonst zu sehr abgeschwächt würde. Einige Wandleuchten sind mit einem ausziehbaren Arm ausgestattet. An beiden Seiten des Spiegels angebracht, lässt sich so die Richtung des Lichteinfalls je nach Bedarf verändern. Aus Sicherheitsgründen ist von Hängelampen und ungeschützten Glühbirnen abzuraten. In der Nasszone, d. h. im Bereich der Badewanne oder der Dusche, ist eine Beleuchtung normalerweise nicht notwendig, da die allgemeine Lichtquelle auch diesen Bereich ausreichend abdeckt. Es ist möglich, zusätzlich eine indirekte Lichtquelle anzubringen, um so eine wärmere Atmosphäre zu erzeugen. Für diese Fälle sollte man jedoch wasserdichte Sicherheitsstrahler, oder auch mit Glasschirmen geschützte Halogenstrahler wählen. Im allgemeinen benötigt auch der Bereich mit den sanitären Anlagen keine eigene Lichtquelle. Generell ist es jedoch möglich, bestimmte Bereiche des Badezimmers durch einen auf den jeweiligen Bereich gerichteten Wandstrahler hervorzuheben. So schaffen z. B. Wandstrahler, die über Gemälden angebracht werden, ein individuelleres Ambiente.

L'ÉCLAIRAGE DE LA SALLE DE BAINS

La lumière la meilleure dans la salle de bains est la lumière naturelle, du fait qu'elle ne fausse pas les couleurs. Cela facilite les tâches demandant une certaine précision comme le maquillage et le rasage. Dans les salles de bains ayant des fenêtres il faut éviter les rideaux, les stores ou les vitres trop opaques qui empêchent à la lumière de pénétrer. Les rideaux de voile et les verres translucides permettent de maintenir une certaine intimité sans être un obstacle à la lumière. Même en ayant une pièce très lumineuse, il est nécessaire de prévoir avec soin les points de lumière artificielle employés à la tombée du jour. On a besoin d'une lumière chaude et uniforme. L'installation de plusieurs lampes halogènes au plafond est une bonne solution. Ce type d'éclairage donne une lumière blanche très semblable à la lumière naturelle. En plus de l'éclairage général, la zone da la table de toilette demande une attention particulière. Deux appliques placées des deux cotés ou à la partie supérieure du miroir donnent une lumière correcte et permettent d'éclairer le visage de façon homogène. Une autre solution étant des points de lumière placés au-dessus du miroir en évitant que la lumière ne s'y reflète pour empêcher un jeux de lumière désavantageux. Les appliques doivent avoir un abat-jour résistant aux vapeurs d'eau (on doit éviter les matériaux naturels non traités), et ils ne doivent être ni trop foncés ni de couleur trop intense pour ne pas fausser la lumière. Il existe des appliques à bras extensibles qui mises côte à côte permettent de changer la direction de la lumière en fonction de la nécessité. Pour des raisons de sécurité il est déconseillé d'utiliser des lampes qui ne sont pas protégées par un abat-jour ou qui pendent. L'éclairage de la zone d'eau (baignoire et douche) n'est pas nécessaire l'éclairage général placé au plafond étant suffisant. Si on le désire on peut y ajouter une lumière indirecte pour créer une atmosphère plus chaude et relaxante. Si on choisi cette solution, il est bon de choisir des lampes étanches de sécurité spécialement destinée à supporter un contact direct avec l'eau, ou des lampes halogènes protégées par un verre. En général la zone des sanitaires n'a pas besoin non plus d'éclairage propre. De toute manière si on désire que l'un des coins de la salle de bains se détache particulièrement, on peut installer des appliques dirigées directement sur cet endroit. Un tableau mis sous verre et éclairé par des appliques fixées au-dessus, donne une atmosphère très personnelle à la salle de bains.

LA ILUMINACIÓN EN EL BAÑO

La mejor luz en el cuarto de baño es, sin duda, la natural, puesto que no desvirtúa los colores y facilita las tareas que requieren mayor precisión, como el maquillaje o el afeitado. Los baños con ventanas deben evitar cortinas, estores o cristales demasiado opacos que desaprovechan la iluminación del exterior. Telas finas y vidrios translúcidos pueden mantener la intimidad sin ser obstáculo del paso de la luz. Aun teniendo un espacio muy luminoso, deben preverse los distintos puntos de luz artificial para cuando cae el día. El cuarto de baño necesita un tipo de luz general cálida y uniforme, por lo que una buena opción es instalar diversos focos halógenos repartidos por el techo. Este tipo de iluminación produce una luz blanca, muy parecida a la natural. Además de la iluminación general, la zona del tocador requiere de una atención especial. Dos apliques en los extremos superiores del espejo o a los lados consiguen una correcta iluminación y logran que el rostro se ilumine de forma homogénea. Otra opción son luces alineadas sobre el espejo, siempre que la claridad no se refleje directamente sobre él para evitar molestos reflejos que deslumbren. Los apliques deben tener una pantalla resistente al vapor del agua (deben evitarse materiales naturales sin tratar) y sus pantallas no han de ser muy opacas ni de un color demasiado intenso, puesto que desvirtuarían la luz. Existen apliques con brazo extensible que, colocados a ambos lados del espejo, permiten modificar la dirección de la luz en función de las necesidades. Por cuestiones de seguridad, no son aconsejables bombillas que no estén protegidas con pantallas o utilizar lámparas colgantes. La iluminación en la zona de aguas (bañera o ducha) no es necesaria, puesto que la luz general del baño (los focos empotrados en el techo) ya ilumina esta zona. Si se desea, puede añadirse una luz indirecta para crear un ambiente más cálido y relajante. Si se elige esta opción, deben utilizarse focos estancos de seguridad especialmente diseñados para soportar el contacto directo con el agua, o bien focos halógenos protegidos con pantallas de cristal. Por norma general, la zona de los sanitarios tampoco dispone de luz propia. De todas maneras, si se desea destacar algún rincón del baño puede instalarse un aplique con luz dirigida hacia esa zona concreta. Unos apliques situados encima de unos cuadros (protegidos con cristal) en el baño, por ejemplo, consiguen un ambiente más personalizado.

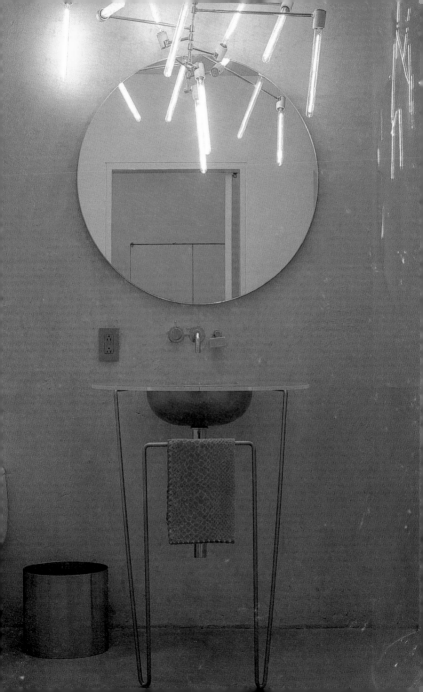

BATHROOM AND AC

Sanitaires et accessoires de salles de bains
Sanitäre Einrichtungen und Zubehörteile für das Bad
FITTINGS
CESSORIES
Sanitarios y complementos de baño

BATHTUBS

On the market today can be found a wide variety of bathtub models, from cutting-edge designs to classical style to modern versions with traditional bases. The standard measurement for a conventional bathtub is 1.60 cm or 1.70 cm long x 70 cm wide. Smaller models (1.40 cm or 1.20 cm long x 70 cm wide) are designed for more limited spaces. Even models smaller than this are manufactured and can be situated just about anywhere. Most bathtubs are made of acrylic and methacrylate materials, as these substances are resistant, maintain temperature very well and permit a wide array of designs. Other materials used are cast iron, which is highly resistant, and steel sheets, which are lighter in structure. Hydrotherapy bathtubs measure the same as conventional models but differ with respect to the features they offer. The interior of a hydrotherapy tub contains a series of jets (usually manipulable) that produce different types of massages. The water massage consists of the release of pressure in the form of a water jet, with a variable proportion of air. The water-air massage combines the propulsion of these two elements. The system of ultrasound massage, the most innovative, involves an integral massage through sound waves. The most innovative designs allow the user to program the desired massage through digital screens that regulate temperature and duration and incorporate self-cleaning mechanisms. Water massage bathtubs are increasingly silent and innovative. Many companies offer combined bathtub-shower models with a steam bath option.

BADEWANNEN

Auf dem Sektor der Badewannen bietet der Markt eine breite Angebotspalette an Modellen, angefangen bei avantgardistischen Designs, über klassische Stile bis hin zu modernen Versionen traditioneller Formen mit antikisierenden Füßen. Die Standartmaße einer herkömmlichen rechteckigen Badewanne betragen 160 cm oder 170 cm in der Länge und 70 cm in der Breite. Darüber hinaus gibt es reduzierte Modelle (140 cm oder 120 cm lang und 70 cm breit), die sich an Räume von geringer Größe anpassen, bis hin zu noch kleineren Badewannen, die in alle Ecken hineinpassen. Die meisten Badewannen sind aus Acryl oder Metaacrylat hergestellt, da diese Materialien widerstandsfähig sind, Temperaturen sehr gut halten und große Variationsmöglichkeiten im Design erlauben. Ebenfalls Verwendung finden das sehr haltbare Gusseisen oder leichtere Stahlplatten. Badewannen mit Unterwassermassage haben die gleiche Größe wie die herkömmlichen Modelle, unterscheiden sich aber in den Leistungen, die sie anbieten. Im Inneren weisen sie eine Reihe von (normalerweise verstellbaren) Düsen auf, die verschiedene Formen von Massagen erzeugen können. Die Unterwassermassage setzt unter großem Druck einen Wasserstrahl frei, dessen Luftbeimischung variabel ist. Die Wasser- und Luftmassage kombiniert das Verfahren dieser beiden Formen und das System der Ultraschallmassage, das innovativste in diesem Bereich, erzeugt eine vollständige Massage mittels Schallwellen. Die neuesten Entwicklungen auf diesem Gebiet erlauben dem Benutzer die wahlweise Einstellung der Massageart an einem digitalen Bildschirm, der die Temperatur und Dauer reguliert und ein Mechanismus zur automatischen Reinigung beinhaltet. Badewannen mit Unterwassermassagesystem sind leise und neuartig. Viele Firmen bieten sogar Modelle an, die Dusche und Badewanne kombinieren und so ein Dampfbad ermöglichen.

103

LES BAIGNOIRES

Il existe une grande variété de baignoires sur le marché, des modèles actuels ou de style classique, jusqu'aux versions modernes au design typique de baignoires antiques sur pieds. Les dimensions standard d'une baignoire conventionnelle rectangulaire sont de 1,60 m - 1,70 m de long sur 0,7 m de large, bien qu'il en existe également de taille plus petite s'adaptant aux espaces plus réduits (1,40 m - 1,20 m sur 0,70 m), certaines étant même de moindre dimension et pouvant être installées dans n'importe quel recoin. La plupart des baignoires sont en matière acrylique ou méthacryliques résistantes, conservant bien la chaleur et offrant toute une variété de design. D'autres matériaux utilisés sont la fonte, très résistante, ou l'acier qui est beaucoup plus léger. Les baignoires à hydromassage ont les mêmes dimensions que les autres, se différenciant pourtant par les prestations qu'elles offrent. Elles ont des jets incorporés (généralement orientables) permettant différents types de massages : celui de l'eau consiste à la propulser sous pression d'un jet d'eau en y ajoutant une proportion variable d'air ; le massage d'eau et d'air combine la propulsion de ces deux éléments. Le système à ultrasons, le plus innovateur, consiste à créer un massage intégral au moyen d'ondes. Le dernier cri en ce qui concerne ce type de baignoires permet de programmer le massage choisi à l'aide d'un panneau digital réglant la température et la durée et disposant d'un système auto-nettoyant incorporé. Elles sont de plus en plus silencieuses et novatrices. Plusieurs maisons offrent des systèmes combinés de baignoires et douches permettant de prendre des bains de vapeur.

BAÑERAS

En el mercado existe una gran variedad de modelos de bañeras, de formas muy actuales o de estilo clásico, incluso versiones modernas de los típicos diseños con patas de antaño. Las medidas estándar de una bañera convencional rectangular son entre 1,60 cm y 1,70 cm de largo por 70 cm de ancho, aunque existen modelos más reducidos que se adaptan a espacios más pequeños (1,40-1,20 x 70 cm), e incluso algunas todavía más reducidas que pueden colocarse en cualquier rincón. La mayoría de las bañeras se fabrica con materiales acrílicos o metacrilato, puesto que son resistentes, mantienen muy bien la temperatura y permiten gran variedad de diseños. Otros materiales utilizados son el hierro fundido, muy resistente, o las planchas de acero, más ligeras. Las bañeras de hidromasaje miden lo mismo que las convencionales, pero se diferencian de ellas por las prestaciones que ofrecen. Incorporan en su interior una serie de válvulas (normalmente orientables) que pueden producir diferentes tipos de masaje: el de agua consiste en la salida a presión de un chorro con una proporción variable de aire; el masaje de agua y aire combina la propulsión de estos dos elementos, y el sistema de ultrasonidos, el más moderno, consiste en crear un masaje integral mediante ondas. Las propuestas más innovadoras en cuanto al tipo de bañera permiten programar el tipo de masaje elegido mediante pantallas digitales que regulan la temperatura y la duración e incorporan sistemas de autolimpieza. Las bañeras de hidromasaje son cada vez más silenciosas e innovadoras. Muchas firmas ofrecen estructuras combinadas de bañera y ducha que permiten disfrutar de baños de vapor.

SHOWERS

While the shower is a practical alternative in bathrooms with limited space, it also is appropriate for large spaces. The shower base should have a minimum measurement of 60 x 60 cm, though the larger it is the more comfortable the space will be. There are many designs, adaptable to any space: square bases, rectangular bases, angled bases (for corners), bases with raised borders to keep water from overflowing. The materials used are also quite diverse: tropical wood, marble, acrylics, porcelain, and glass fiber. Some are equipped with specially designed protective surfaces to avoid slips. There are also models with small stools integrated into the structure, allowing the user to sit down while taking a shower.

Like the bathtub, the shower requires a partition in order to avoid splashing and to isolate the bath-shower area from the rest of the bathroom. Glass (transparent or acid-treated) is the most commonly used material for affecting this separation. There exist multiple designs for each model of shower: sliding doors or panels, folding leaves, magnetic shutters, etc. Some prefabricated shower stalls—with base and partition included—are equipped with a water massage shower and a sauna, among other functions. For smaller bathrooms, columns are a good alternative to stalls. They consist of small panels of stainless steel, methacrylate, wood, or glass with a water fixture and several jets. This alternative permits equal enjoyment of a water massage and can be integrated within a normal shower base or a bathtub.

DUSCHEN

Die Dusche ist eine gelungene Alternative für Badezimmer mit wenig Platz, obwohl sie auch in große Bäder eingebaut werden kann. Die Wanne der Dusche sollte eine Mindestgröße von 60 cm x 60 cm haben, wobei als Grundregel gilt: je größer desto bequemer. Das Angebot ist vielfältig und kann an alle Räumlichkeiten angepasst werden: Es gibt Duschen in quadratischer, rechteckiger und über Eck gehender Form, genauso wie Duschbecken mit hochgezogenen Rändern, um das Überlaufen von Wasser zu vermeiden. Die verwendeten Materialien sind sehr unterschiedlich: tropische Hölzer, Marmor, Acrylstoffe, Porzellan, Glasfaser, ... Einige von ihnen sind mit speziell entwickelten Oberflächen ausgestattet, die ein Ausrutschen verhindern. Es gibt sogar Modelle mit kleinen eingebauten Hockern, die es dem Benutzer erlauben, sich während des Duschens zu setzen.

Wie die Badewanne benötigt auch die Dusche einen Aufsatz zum Schutz gegen Spritzwasser, der den Duschbereich vom übrigen Badezimmer abtrennt. Durchsichtiges oder mit Säure behandeltes Glas ist das am meisten verwandte Material für diese Trennwände, die in zahllosen Designs für jede Art von Dusche angeboten werden: als Schiebe- oder Flügeltüren, Falttüren, mit Magnetverschlüssen, usw. ... Einige vorgefertigte Duschen (inklusive Duschwanne und -aufsatz) bieten neben anderen Funktionen auch eine Wassermassage und Sauna an. Bei Bädern mit sehr eingeschränktem Platz sind Duschsäulen eine geeignete Alternative zu Duschkabinen. Sie bestehen aus kleinen Paneelen aus rostfreiem Edelstahl, Metaacrylat, Holz oder Glas und sind mit Armaturen und mehreren Düsen versehen. Dies ermöglicht dem Benutzer ebenfalls den Genuss einer Wassermassage und kann sowohl in eine herkömmliche Dusche als auch Badewanne integriert werden.

LES DOUCHES

La douche représente une bonne alternative pour de petites salles de bains, tout en pouvant être placée dans des espaces plus grands. Le plateau de douche doit avoir une taille minimum de 60 x 60 cm. Quoique, plus il est grand plus il est agréable. Il en existe une grande diversité s'adaptant à tous les espaces : des plateaux de douches carrés, rectangulaires, angulaires (très utiles dans les coins) avec des rebords (empêchant l'eau de déborder) … Les matériaux employés sont très divers : bois tropicaux, marbre, matériaux acryliques, porcelaine, fibre de verre … Certains présentent une surface rugueuse évitant de glisser. Certains modèles existent également avec des petits tabourets intégrés permettant de s'asseoir en prenant sa douche.

La douche, de même que la baignoire, requiert un pare-douche afin de se protéger des éclaboussures et séparer la zone d'eau du reste de la salle de bains. Le verre, transparent ou mat, est le plus courant pour ce type de séparation. Il existe divers modèles pour chaque design : à portes coulissantes, battantes ou pliantes, avec fermetures magnétiques etc. Certaines cabines de douches préfabriquées proposent, entre autres fonctions, jets hydromasseurs et sauna intégrés. Pour les petits espaces, les colonnes sont une bonne alternative aux cabines. Il s'agit de petits panneaux en acier inoxydable, méthacryliques, en bois ou en verres où sont incorporés les robinets et différents jets d'eau. Ils permettent de jouir également d'un hydromassage et peuvent être placés dans une douche conventionnelle ou une baignoire.

DUCHAS

La ducha es una buena alternativa en baños que no disponen de suficientes metros, pero también puede colocarse en grandes espacios. El plato de ducha debe tener unas medidas mínimas de 60 x 60 cm, aunque cuanto más grande sea más cómodo resultará. Existen múltiples propuestas que se adaptan a cualquier espacio: platos de ducha cuadrados, rectangulares, en forma de ángulo (para aprovechar un rincón), con faldones (para que el agua no se desborde)... Los materiales empleados son muy diversos: madera tropical, mármol, materiales acrílicos, porcelana, fibra de vidrio... algunos de ellos ofrecen superficies tramadas para evitar resbalones. Incluso hay modelos que incorporan pequeños taburetes integrados en la estructura y que permiten sentarse mientras se toma una ducha. La ducha, al igual que la bañera, precisa una mampara para evitar las salpicaduras y aislar la zona de aguas del resto del baño. El cristal transparente o al ácido es el material más utilizado para esta separación. Hay múltiples modelos para cada diseño: puertas correderas o batientes, hojas plegables, cierres magnéticos, etc... Algunas cabinas de ducha prefabricadas –con plato y mampara incluidos– ofrecen ducha de hidromasaje y sauna, entre otras funciones. Para baños con menos espacio, las columnas son una buena alternativa a las cabinas de ducha. Se trata de pequeños paneles realizados en acero inoxidable, metacrilato, madera o cristal que incorporan una grifería y varios jets. Permiten disfrutar igualmente del sistema de hidromasaje y pueden colocarse sobre un plato de ducha convencional o sobre una bañera.

TOILETS

A wide range of designs, materials and colors apply to contemporary toilet and bidet models. When selecting these fittings it is important to consider the style of the bathroom, as well as the advantages they offer and the materials of which they consist. Porcelain is the most frequently used material since it is sturdy and resistant to the passage of time; though more cutting-edge stainless steel models are also on the market. Many companies manufacture a matching toilet-bidet-sink ensemble, yet there are no fixed rules prohibiting combination of distinct designs and materials. In any case, the most conventional approach is to select the same model of toilet and bidet, as they will be situated side by side. It is advisable that they have similar proportions. If the sink is to be placed in another part of the bathroom (the bath-shower area), selecting a different style is more conducive. Fittings with a base are the most classical design and have only one potential drawback: the cement of the base joints must be securely fixed in order to avoid structural instability. Fittings without a base or suspended fittings are less voluminous and more difficult to install. Yet, they are an effective means of taking maximum advantage of available space. The fittings should be installed in close proximity to the drainpipes. A minimum of 25 cm should separate the toilet from the bidet.

TOILETTEN

Ein großes Spektrum an Designmöglichkeiten, Materialien und Farben kennzeichnet die aktuelle Angebotspalette von Wasserklosetts und Bidets. Bei ihrer Auswahl ist es von großer Wichtigkeit, den Stils des Badezimmers zu berücksichtigen ebenso wie die Vorteile des Modells und die Materialien, aus denen es gefertigt wurde. Porzellan ist das am meisten benutzte Material, da es strapazierfähig und sehr lange haltbar ist, auch wenn heute einige sehr viel modernere Modelle aus rostfreiem Stahl vermarktet werden. Viele Firmen stellen aufeinander abgestimmte Ensembles aus Toilette, Bidet und Waschbecken her, obwohl es keine festen Regeln für Kombinationen gibt und man verschiedene Designs und Materialien durchaus mischen kann. Im Allgemeinen ist es üblich Toilette und Bidet aus der gleichen Modellreihe zu wählen, da sie normalerweise nebeneinander platziert werden und es ist ratsam, dass beide Gegenstände ähnliche Proportionen haben. Da das Waschbecken in einem anderen Bereich des Badezimmers (dem Platz des Toilettentisches) platziert wird, ist es wesentlich einfacher sich hier für einen anderen Stil zu entscheiden. Die klassischste Toilettenform ist die auf dem Boden stehende, die nur einen Nachteil hat: Der Zement der Bodenfuge muss fest fixiert sein, um eine Instabilität des Gerätes zu verhindern. Toiletten ohne Sockel oder Unterbau sind weniger voluminös und erfordern einen komplizierteren Einbau, erweisen sich aber als gute Wahl zur optimalen Ausnutzung des vorhandenen Platzes. Toiletten sollten im Badezimmers in der Nähe des Abflussrohres platziert sein und zwischen Klosett und Bidet sollte ein Mindestabstand von 25 cm eingehalten werden.

TOILETTES

Pour les toilettes et les bidets, existe tout un éventail de designs, de matériaux et de couleurs. En les choisissant, on les adapte au style de la salle de bains. Mais il est également important de prendre conscience des avantages qu'ils offrent et des matériaux avec lesquels ils sont fabriqués. La porcelaine est le matériel le plus utilisé. Solide et résistant bien au passage du temps, bien qu'aujourd'hui on trouve également des modèles en acier inoxydable beaucoup plus modernes. Beaucoup de maisons fabriquent des jeux de modèles comprenant toilettes, bidet et lavabo, bien qu'il soit également possible de combiner différents designs et matériaux. En général, il est normal de choisir le même modèle pour les toilettes et le bidet. Du fait qu'ils sont généralement placés l'un à côté de l'autre, il est préférable qu'ils aient des proportions semblables. Le lavabo étant situé à un autre endroit de la salle de bains (côté coiffeuse), il est plus facile de le choisir d'un autre style. Les sanitaires à pieds sont les plus classiques et ne présentent qu'un handicap, le fait que la jointure en ciment doit être bien fixée afin d'éviter une instabilité de la pièce. Les sanitaires sans pieds ou suspendus sont moins volumineux et requièrent une installation plus complexe, mais représentent une bonne solution pour jouir au maximum de l'espace donné. Les sanitaires doivent être placés à proximité des tuyaux d'évacuation des eaux et le bidet et les toilettes doivent être séparés de 25 cm au minimum.

SANITARIOS

Un gran abanico de diseños, materiales y colores conforman los modelos actuales de inodoros y bidés. Para elegirlos es importante valorar el estilo del cuarto de baño, pero también hay que pensar en las ventajas que ofrecen y los materiales con que están fabricados. La porcelana es el material más utilizado porque es sufrido y resiste bien el paso del tiempo, aunque en la actualidad se comercializan algunos modelos en acero inoxidable, mucho más actual. Muchas firmas fabrican un modelo a juego para inodoro, bidé y lavamanos, aunque no hay reglas fijas y pueden mezclarse diseños y materiales distintos. De todas formas, lo más normal es elegir un mismo modelo para inodoro y bidé, puesto que se sitúan uno al lado del otro y es aconsejable que tengan proporciones semejantes. Al situarse el lavamanos en otra parte del baño (la zona del tocador), es más fácil elegir otro estilo. Los sanitarios con pie son los más clásicos y presentan sólo un inconveniente: el cemento de las juntas del pie debe estar bien fijado para evitar la inestabilidad de la pieza. Los sanitarios sin pie o suspendidos son menos voluminosos y necesitan una instalación más compleja, pero son una buena opción para aprovechar al máximo el espacio. Los sanitarios deben colocarse muy cerca del bajante de aguas, y entre el inodoro y el bidé debe haber, como mínimo, 25 cm de separación.

SINKS

Among the various fittings, sinks offer the most diverse possibilities. Sinks are an essential piece in the bathroom ensemble. While certain models seek to optimize space (some are as small as 30 cm in diameter), others include a built-in cabinet to store towels. Sinks with a pedestal recreate classical models and are often sold to match the toilet and bidet. More innovative designs often have a counter, are built into a furniture piece, or are freestanding. Oval, rectangular, square and cylindrical forms, as well as materials as diverse as porcelain, glass, stainless steel and synthetic material, characterize the wide range of sinks on the market today. If one does not to opt for a uniform sink and counter structure, it is important to choose a counter piece that goes well with the lavatory and is highly resistant. Marble confers a more classical and elegant style. Wood, in all its variants, is another option. There are tropical woods such as bubinga or wengue, or clearer woods such as natural maple or beech. Much in vogue are counters made of synthetic materials, allowing for very attractive and original designs. Glass counters are very light, ideal for small bathrooms. Also available are matted glass counters, transparent counters, and acid-treated counters. Some models allow for the inclusion of a furniture piece below the sink. This type of furniture is made of water-resistant materials (wood, glass, ratan, etc) and is designed take maximum advantage of storage space.

WASCHBECKEN

Waschbecken sind sanitäre Einrichtungen, die einen wesentlichen Bestandteil des Bades bilden und vielfältige Möglichkeiten eröffnen: Einige Modelle nutzen den ihm gegebenen Raum optimal aus (die kleinsten Varianten haben einen Durchmesser von 30 cm), andere sind mit einem Einbauschrank verbunden, um Handtücher aufzubewahren. Waschbecken mit Sockel nehmen klassische Modelle wieder auf und werden normalerweise passend zu Toilette und Bidet verkauft. Neuere Designs hingegen beinhalten manchmal eine Ablagefläche, sind in ein Möbelstück eingebaut oder freistehend. Ovale, rechteckige, quadratische oder zylindrische Formen und so verschiedenartige Materialien wie Porzellan, Glas, rostfreies Edelstahl und synthetische Stoffe charakterisieren die breite Angebotspalette. Wenn man sich nicht für ein Waschbecken mit integrierter Ablage entscheidet, ist es wichtig, dass diese Ablage gut zum übrigen Stil des Badezimmers passt und zugleich sehr widerstandsfähig ist. Sie kann aus Marmor bestehen, dem klassischen und elegantesten Material, und aus Holz in allen seinen Varianten: tropischen Hölzern wie Bubinga oder Wengúe, oder helleren Hölzern wie Naturahorn oder Buche. Ablagen aus neuen synthetischen Materialien sind zur Zeit sehr in Mode, da sie sehr attraktive und originelle Gestaltungsmöglichkeiten bieten. Glasablagen dagegen sind sehr leicht und ideal für kleinere Bäder. Es gibt sie unter anderem in matter Ausführung, durchsichtig oder mit Säure behandelt. Es existieren auch Waschbeckenmodelle, die es erlauben unterhalb ein Möbel einzufügen. Diese Möbel sind aus wasserbeständigen Materialien wie Glas, Holz, Ratan, ... hergestellt und kreative Erfindungen zur optimalen Nutzung des Aufbewahrungsplatzes.

LES LAVABOS

Pour les sanitaires, les lavabos offrent de multiples possibilités et sont l'une des pièces les plus importante de la salle de bains. Certains modèles prennent beaucoup de place (les plus petits ont 30 cm de diamètre), d'autres comprennent une armoire encastrée permettant de ranger les serviettes de bains. Ceux sur pied sont les plus classiques et viennent en général vendus conjointement avec les toilettes et le bidet. Les modèles plus récents ont un pourtour ou sont encastrés dans un meuble. Ils sont de forme ovale, rectangulaire, carrée ou cylindrique et en matériaux divers ainsi la porcelaine, le verre, l'acier inoxydable et les matériaux synthétiques offrant par la même une très vaste gamme de modèles. Si l'on opte pas pour une lavabo avec pourtour d'une pièce, il est important de choisir un pourtour permettant d'être bien combiné avec celui-ci, et qui soit résistant. Il en existe en marbre, qui lui confère un style classique et élégant, en bois avec toutes ses variantes : bois tropicaux tels que le bubinga ou le wengué ou bois plus claires comme l'érable ou le hêtre. Les pourtours réalisés avec les nouveaux matériaux synthétiques sont très en vogue et permettent de réaliser des designs très attrayants et originaux. Les pourtours de verre sont très légers et idéals pour les petites salles de bains. Ils sont en verre transparent, mat ou traités à l'acide … Certains modèles sont encastrés dans un meuble. Ce type de meuble est réalisé avec des matériaux résistant à l'eau et avec des idées très pratiques pour employer l'espace et permettre de ranger le maximum de choses. Ils sont en bois en verre en osier…

LAVABOS

Los lavabos son sanitarios que ofrecen múltiples posibilidades y constituyen una pieza esencial en el cuarto de baño: algunos modelos aprovechan al máximo el espacio (hay modelos mínimos de 30 cm de diámetro) y otros incluyen un armario empotrado para almacenar toallas. Los de pedestal son los que recrean modelos más clásicos y suelen venderse a juego con el inodoro y el bidé, aunque los diseños más innovadores suelen tener una encimera, empotrar un mueble o bien colocarse exentos. Formas ovaladas, rectangulares, cuadradas, cilíndricas y materiales tan diversos como la porcelana, el cristal, el acero inoxidable y los materiales sintéticos conforman la extensa gama de modelos. Si no se opta por un diseño de lavamanos y encimera de una sola pieza, es importante elegir una encimera que combine bien con el sanitario y que, a la vez, sea muy resistente. Las hay de mármol, que confieren un estilo más clásico y elegante, y de madera, en todas sus variantes: maderas tropicales como la bubinga o el wengué, o maderas más claras, como el arce natural y el haya. Las encimeras fabricadas con los nuevos materiales de síntesis están muy en boga, puesto que permiten hacer diseños muy atractivos y originales. Las encimeras de cristal son muy ligeras, ideales para baños pequeños. Hay encimeras de cristal mate, transparente, al ácido... Existen modelos que permiten incluir un mueble bajolavabo. Este tipo de mobiliario se fabrica con materiales resistentes al agua y con ideas prácticas para aprovechar al máximo el espacio de almacenamiento: de madera, de cristal, de ratán...

BATHROOM FIXTURES AND ACCESSORIES

Fixtures are fundamental bathroom pieces, perfectly adaptable to the various possibilities for sinks, bathtubs and showers. The most common fixture nowadays is the stylized mixer tap for both the boudoir and bath-shower zone. There are also models with a revolving faucet, mixing faucet mixer and double faucets with chrome or satin finish. Some contemporary models take inspiration from antique fixtures, and the most cutting-edge designs include long, curved faucets. Bathroom accessories are indispensable to defining the style of the bathroom and provide the final decorative touch. There also are accessories sets that consist of soap dispensers, soap dishes and toothbrush holders of the same material: glass, bright chrome, or wood. Other accessories such as toilet brushes, toilet-paper racks, shelves, hooks for hanging objects, mirrors and small carts also are essential to the bathroom. Most accessories offer a meticulous aesthetic while at the same fulfilling a practical function. An example is the towel radiator which, along with being aesthetically appealing, allows for towels to be dried after bathing. Wood, porcelain and gilded accessories are ideal choices for recreating a classical ambience, while chrome and glass finish are perfect for bathrooms with an avant-garde aesthetic. Natural floral details, towels, soaps and perfumes provide freshness and add elegance and distinction to the bathroom.

ARMATUREN UND ZUBEHÖRTEILE IM BAD

Armaturen sind wesentliche Bestandteile des Bades, die sich perfekt an die vielfältigen Designmöglichkeiten von Waschbecken, Toiletten und Duschen anpassen sollen. Die heute im Badezimmer gebräuchlichste ist ein einarmiger Wasserhahn in stilisierter Form, der für beide Bereiche (Toilette und Dusch- bzw. Badebereich) benutzt wird. Andere Modelle haben einen drehbaren Wasserhahn, einarmige Mischbatterien, doppelte Hähne mit satinierter oder verchromter Oberfläche ... Einige der zeitgenössischen Modelle sind von antiken Armaturen inspiriert und die fortschrittlichsten Designs zeigen lange und geschwungene Wasserhähne. Die Zubehörteile sind unabdingbar für die Definition des Stils eines Badezimmers und geben ihm seine entscheidende dekorative Note. Es gibt aufeinander abgestimmte Zubehörsets, bestehend aus Seifenspender, Seifenschale und Zahnputzbechern in ein und dem selben Material: Glas, Chrom, Holz, ... Weitere Accessoires wie Klobürsten, Halter für das Toilettenpapier, Regale, Kleiderhacken, Spiegel oder rollbare Hilfswägelchen sind ebenfalls unerlässlich für eine gelungene Badezimmereinrichtung. Die Mehrzahl dieser Dinge verbindet eine äußerst praktische Funktion mit ausgefeilter Ästhetik. Dies zeigt zum Beispiel der sehr dekorative Handtuchheizkörper, der das Trocknen von Handtüchern nach dem Baden ermöglicht. Holz, Porzellan und vergoldetes Zubehör sind die idealen Komponenten zur Schaffung eines klassischen Ambientes, während Oberflächen aus Chrom und Glas dem Badezimmer einen eher avantgardistischen Charakter geben. Details wie natürliche Blumen, Handtücher, Seifen und Parfümfläschchen verbreiten Frische und geben den Bädern ihre Eleganz und ein persönliches Flair.

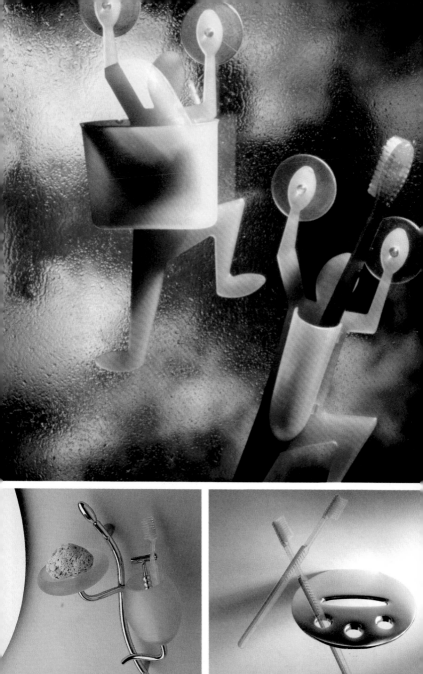

LA ROBINETTERIE ET LES ACCESSOIRES DE LA SALLE DE BAINS

Les robinets sont des pièces essentielles devant s'adapter aux diverses options de design choisies pour les sanitaires. Le plus courant aujourd'hui est un robinet à un bras de forme stylisée aussi bien pour le lavabo que pour la douche et la baignoire. Modèles giratoires, mélangeurs à un bras, à deux robinets, satinés ou chromés … Certains modèles actuels s'inspirent de la robinetterie antique et les plus modernes ont des bras plus longs et recourbés. Les accessoires sont indispensables pour déterminer le style de la salle de bain et lui donner sa touche finale. Il y a des jeux d'accessoires composés de distributeur de savon, de savonnière, de verre à brosse à dents, réalisés dans un même matériel : verre, chrome, bois … D'autres tels que brosses W.C. ou porte-rouleaux, étagère, miroir, petit chariot roulant sont également nécessaire. La plupart des accessoires joignent la fonctionnalité à l'esthétique. Les radiateurs en sont le meilleur exemple pour les serviettes de bain. Ils sont très décoratifs et permettent de sécher les linges après le bain. Le bois, la porcelaine et les accessoires dorés sont idéaux pour créer une atmosphère classique, tandis que ceux en chrome et en verre sont plus avant-gardistes et confèrent une atmosphère plus moderne. Certains détails comme des fleurs, des plantes, des serviettes de bain, des savons, des flacons de parfum donnent une certaine fraîcheur et ajoutent élégance et distinction à la salle de bains.

GRIFERÍAS Y COMPLEMENTOS DE BAÑO

Las griferías son piezas básicas que se adaptan a la perfección a las múltiples opciones de lavamanos, baños y duchas. Lo más habitual hoy para el cuarto de baño es un grifo monomando de formas estilizadas para las dos zonas (tocador y zona de aguas). Modelos con caño giratorio, mezcladores monomando, grifos dobles con acabados como el cromo o el satinado... Algunos modelos actuales se inspiran en las griferías antiguas, y los más avanzados diseños ofrecen caños largos y curvados. Los complementos para el baño son indispensables para definir el estilo del cuarto de baño y darle el toque final. Existen juegos de accesorios compuestos por dosificadores de jabón, jaboneras y vasos para cepillos de dientes fabricados con un mismo material: cristal, cromo brillante, madera ... Otros accesorios como escobilleros o portarrollos, estantes o colgadores, espejos o carritos auxiliares también son imprescindibles en el baño. La mayoría de los complementos ofrecen una estética muy cuidada y cumplen, a la vez, una función muy práctica. Muestra de ello son los radiadores-toallero, muy decorativos y que permiten secar las toallas después del baño. La madera, la porcelana y los accesorios dorados son ideales para recrear un ambiente clásico, mientras que los acabados en cromo y cristal resultan especialmente idóneos para baños con estética vanguardista. Detalles con flores naturales, toallas, jabones y botes de perfume dotarán de frescura el ambiente y añadirán elegancia o distinción al baño.

Pro
Projekte
PRO
Proye

ets

ECTS

ctos

Salles de bains classiques et romantiques

Klassische und romantische Badezimmer

CLASSIC AND ROMANTIC BATHROOMS

Baños clásicos y románticos

It is difficult to categorize the bathrooms that are designed nowadays, since interior designers are more and more original all the time, and their work often takes on the appearance of an exclusive work of art. At any rate, even those rooms with the greatest personality, get their inspiration from some decorative style, whether it be owing to tiny details, or to the materials chosen as wall or floor coverings. As a general rule, classical bathrooms require large spaces in order to afford maximum elegance and beauty. If the dimensions are large, then it is normal to divide the space into the three main zones: the dressing area, the wet area, and the toilet area. The dressing area, the least intimate of the three, is usually situated near the door. The bathtub or shower area, is usually a bit more reserved. In a classical bathroom with ample space, usually a bathtub is preferred, which is situated in front of, or next to, a window which affords natural light. If space is not so abundant, then light colors will be used. Likewise, a shower may replace the tub, the bidet done away with, and even, the toilet may be affixed to the wall, so as to gain space. Due to its beauty and elegance, marble is the material par excellence for recreating classical style. It is used on the floor, and even for the walls and partitions. Although it is porous and can be easily stained, it is resistant to water and water vapor. If it is used for the floor, it should have a non-slip coating. If a light-colored marble without too much grain is chosen, then it will make the space seem larger. On the other hand, a dark-toned marble will confer distinction and elegance. Moldings, columns and even a classical-style lamp, can completely transform a space. Contemporary bathrooms with a classical air, make use of elements which denote this style: large mirrors with thick ornamental frames, or smaller details such as antique fixtures, or old-style handles or knobs on closets, cabinets or doors, reminiscent of a bygone era.

Salles de bains
classiques et
romantiques
Klassische und romantische
Badezimmer

CLASSIC AND
ROMANTIC
BATHROOMS

Baños clásicos
y románticos

Heutzutage entworfene Bäder bestimmten Stilrichtungen zuzuordnen ist kein leichtes Unterfangen, denn die Originalität der Innenarchitekten kennt keine Grenzen und oftmals scheint jede Kreation ein exklusives Einzelstück. Dessen ungeachtet sind selbst persönlich gestaltete Räume an einen bestimmten Dekorationsstil angelehnt – sei es durch kleine Details oder aufgrund der für die Verkleidung von Böden und Wänden gewählten Materialien. Im Allgemeinen erfordern Bäder im klassischen Stil große Räume, um ihre Schönheit und Eleganz voll entfalten zu können. Verfügt das Bad über großzügige Maße, erfolgt typischerweise eine praktische Unterteilung in die drei Hauptbereiche des Badezimmers: den Waschtischbereich, den Nassbereich und den Toilettenbereich. Der Waschtisch liegt der Eingangstür am nächsten, da er am wenigsten der Privatsphäre bedarf. Badewanne oder Dusche ist ein intimerer Bereich vorbehalten. In der Regel entscheidet man sich bei einem geräumigen klassischen Badezimmer dafür, eine Badewanne von großen Abmessungen nach Möglichkeit gegenüber oder neben einem Fenster zu platzieren, durch das reichlich Tageslicht einströmt. Falls nicht so viel Raum vorhanden ist, kann die Badewanne durch eine Dusche ersetzt werden, wobei helle Materialien verwendet werden. Im Toilettenbereich empfiehlt sich ein Verzicht auf das Bidet und eine Konzentration ausschließlich auf das WC, das zudem, an die Wand gehängt, Platz spart. Das mit dem klassischen Stil verbundene Material par excellence ist der Marmor – stets von großer Schönheit und Eleganz. Er wird für Böden, Wände sowie kleine Trennwände verwendet. Ein Material, das gegenüber Wasser und Dampf äußerst unempfindlich, jedoch aufgrund seiner Porosität anfällig für Flecken ist. Als Bodenbelag sollte Marmor über eine spezielle Oberflächenbehandlung verfügen, um der Rutschgefahr zu begegnen. Entscheidet man sich für hellen Marmor erscheint der Raum größer; bevorzugt man hingegen einen dunkleren Ton, wirkt das Bad nobel und elegant. Profilleisten, Säulen und selbst eine Lampe im klassischen Stil können einen Raum vollkommen verändern. In den neuesten Badezimmern mit einem gewissen Hauch von Klassik finden sich Elemente, die diesen Stil prägen: große Spiegel mit dicken verzierten Rahmen oder kleinere Details wie alte Armaturen sowie Schränke und Türen mit antiken Griffen, die uns zweifellos in die Vergangenheit zurückversetzen.

Salles de bains classiques et romantiques

Classic and Romantic Bathrooms

KLASSISCHE UND ROMANTISCHE BADEZIMMER

Baños clásicos y romanticos

Il est difficile de classifier les styles de salles de bains crées de nos jours, puisque l'originalité des décorateurs d'intérieur est toujours plus grande et dans beaucoup de cas parait être une création exclusive. De toute façon, même les espaces dotés d'une grande personnalité s'inspirent d'un style de décoration quelconque, que se soit au moyen de petits détails, ou au travers des matériaux choisis pour revêtir sols et parois. En général les salles de bains de style classique nécessitent un espace plus grand pour pouvoir recréer au maximum élégance et beauté. Si la salle de bains est de grande dimension il est facile de la diviser en trois zones principales : celle de la coiffeuse et du lavabo, celle de l'eau (avec la baignoire et/ou la douche) et la zone réservée aux sanitaires. La coiffeuse se trouve à proximité de la porte d'entrée, il s'agit de la partie de la salle de bains qui demande le moins d'intimité. Une zone plus réservée est celle destinée à la baignoire ou à la douche. En général dans une salle de bains classique et ayant suffisamment de place on choisira d'installer une grande baignoire, si possible en face ou à côté d'une fenêtre avec une lumière naturelle abondante. Si on n'a pas suffisamment de place on pourra substituer une douche à la baignoire, de même qu'on emploiera des matériaux claires, et dans la zone des sanitaires on renoncera au bidet au profit des toilettes qui pourront être fixées à la parois, ce qui permettra de gagner de la place. Le matériel qui recrée par excellence le style classique de beauté et d'élégance, est le marbre. On l'utilise pour les sols, les parois et les murs de séparation. C'est un matériel très résistant à l'eau et à la vapeur bien que poreux et se tachant facilement. Pour le sol il est préférable qu'il ait une finition spéciale pour le rendre moins glissant. Si on choisit un marbre clair (et sans trop de veines), l'espace paraîtra plus grand quoique si on préfère un ton plus foncé on obtiendra une salle de bains très distinguée et élégante. Des moulures, des colonnes de même qu'une lampe classique peuvent transformer un espace complètement. Les salles de bains actuelles à tendance classique ajoutent des éléments propres à ce style, tels que de grands miroirs ayant des cadres très ornementés ou d'autres détails tels que des robinets antiques de même que des portes et des armoires avec de vieille poignées et de vieux boutons qui nous transporteront sans aucun doute dans un lointain passé.

Classic and Romantic Bathrooms
Klassische und romantische Badezimmer
SALLES DE BAINS CLASSIQUES ET ROMANTIQUES
Baños clásicos y románticos

Es difícil clasificar en estilos los baños que se proyectan en la actualidad, puesto que la originalidad de los interioristas es cada vez mayor y, en muchos casos, parece como si cada creación fuera obra exclusiva de autor. De todas formas, incluso los espacios dotados de máxima personalidad se inspiran en algún estilo decorativo, ya sea mediante pequeños detalles o a través de los materiales elegidos para revestir suelos y paredes. Por norma general, los baños de estilo clásico requieren grandes espacios para recrear al máximo su elegancia y belleza. Y si el baño es de grandes dimensiones, lo más usual es que puedan dividirse cómodamente las tres zonas principales: la de tocador, la de aguas (con bañera y/o ducha) y la zona reservada a los sanitarios. El tocador se sitúa en la zona más cercana a la puerta de entrada, al tratarse de la parte del baño que precisa menos intimidad. Otra zona, más reservada, es la que se destina a la bañera o a la ducha. Por norma general, un baño clásico con muchos metros opta por la opción de instalar una bañera de grandes proporciones, a ser posible enfrente o junto a una ventana con abundante luz natural. Si no se dispone de tanto espacio, puede sustituirse la bañera por la ducha, además de emplear materiales claros, y en la zona de sanitarios prescindir del bidé y dar protagonismo únicamente al inodoro, que puede suspenderse en la pared para ganar espacio. El material que por excelencia recrea el estilo clásico es el mármol, de gran belleza y elegancia. Se utiliza en suelos e incluso en paredes y muretes de separación. Es un material muy resistente al agua y al vapor, aunque al ser poroso puede mancharse con facilidad. Para el suelo es mejor que el mármol tenga un acabado especial para que no se haga resbaladizo. Si se elige un mármol claro (y sin demasiadas vetas) el espacio parecerá aún mayor, aunque si se prefiere un tono más oscuro, se recreará un baño muy distinguido y elegante. Molduras, columnas e incluso una lámpara de estilo clásico pueden transformar completamente un espacio. Los baños más actuales con cierto aire clásico incorporan elementos que marcan este estilo: grandes espejos de gruesos marcos ornamentados o detalles más menudos como griferías o pomos antiguos en armarios y puertas que nos remiten, sin duda, a un pasado remoto.

Salles de bains
classiques et
romantiques
Klassische und romantische
Badezimmer
BAÑOS CLÁSICOS
Y ROMÁNTICOS
*Classic and
Romantic Bathrooms*

Classique en marbre
Klassisch in Marmor
MARBLE CLASSIC
Clásico en mármol

Photo © Jordi Miralles

Hommage à l'antique
Hommage an die Antike
A TRIBUTE TO
THE ANTIQUE
Homenaje a lo antiguo

Simple et sobre
Einfach und formal
SIMPLE AND FORMAL
Simple y formal

Photo © Lluís Miras

Salles de bains rustiques
Rustikale Badezimmer
RUSTIC
BATHROOMS
Baños rústicos

Traditional rustic style is what is used to define the lifestyle of country homes. It is a lifestyle which recreates a way of life in direct contact with nature. This decorative style is characterized especially by the use of natural, simple materials. Likewise, floors and walls are basically free of ornamentation. Terracota, earthenware or old marble floor tiles are ideal. Marble can be a cold material which may be suitable for classical styles. Nevertheless, if aged marble is used, the effect may be just the opposite, which is to say, it will grant warmth. Wall stuccoing is very common in rural decoration. Apart from conferring a very natural style of decoration, it is very good for combatting humidity. To make the stucco, lime, natural pigments such as oxide, and terracota are used. Striking results with great personality can be achieved such as walls with a red coloring and an aged appearance. Natural materials can be combined, without hesitation, in a rustic bathroom, although, they normally must receive some type of treatment in order to be able to withstand water and dampness. Of course, wood is commonly used, but it had best be given a coating which affords it an aged appearance, so as to confer a more rustic touch. Old, used materials such as beams and wooden flooring, can be used. Likewise, even stone can be used for the walls, or antique troughs as washbasins. Modern-day bathrooms with a rustic air combine the use of contemporary elements with rough and natural materials. A bathtub with feet (many contemporary designs modeled on designs of yesteryear, are available) takes center stage, in a clean, uncluttered space, with diverse types of natural coverings for the walls and floors. Simple shapes are combined with different materials in baths of an almost ecclectic design, although with a touch of rustic inspiration. The colors and rough textures also mark this style. Stone and gray shades on the walls, for the bathtub and for the furniture, grant it an old, traditional air.

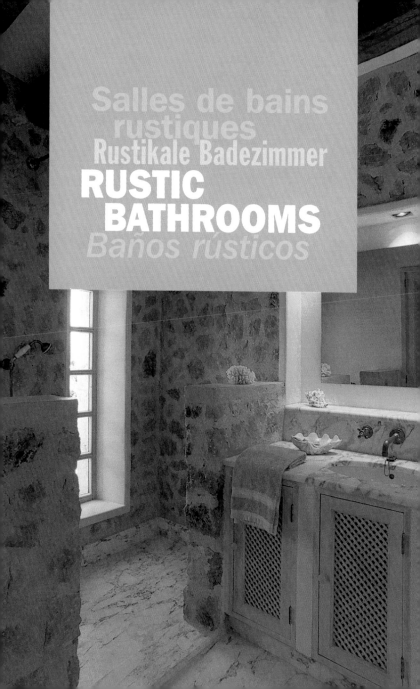

Salles de bains rustiques
Rustikale Badezimmer
RUSTIC BATHROOMS
Baños rústicos

Der traditionelle rustikale Stil (Landhausstil) gilt als Ausdruck des Lebensstils in Landhäusern, die eine in direktem Kontakt mit der Natur stehende Lebensweise widerspiegelt. Hauptmerkmal dieses Dekorationsstils ist die Verwendung natürlicher und schlichter Materialien mit Verzierungen an Böden wie Wänden. Ideal sind Fliesen aus Terrakotta oder gebranntem Ton und Bodenfliesen aus Antikmarmor. Marmor ist ein Material, das kalt wirken und für klassische Umgebungen geeignet sein mag. Entscheidet man sich jedoch für Antikmarmor (vor allem in neutralen und natürlichen Farbtönen), so kann dadurch der entgegengesetzte Effekt erreicht und dem Raum Wärme verliehen werden. Verputzte Wände kommen in ländlichen Umgebungen häufig vor. Sie stellen eine Art des Oberflächenabschlusses dar, der feuchtigkeitsresistent ist und gleichzeitig eine natürliche dekorative Wirkung erzielt. Der Putz besteht aus Kalk und natürlichen Pigmenten wie Rost oder Terrakotta und kann so erstaunliche Oberflächen schaffen – wie farbig gestrichene Wände, die antik wirken und viel Persönlichkeit ausstrahlen. Natürliche Materialien können problemlos in einem Badezimmer im rustikalen Stil miteinander kombiniert werden, wenngleich die Mehrheit von ihnen eine Vorbehandlung erfordert, um durch Wasser und Feuchtigkeit keinen Schaden zu nehmen. Holz ist zweifellos ein weiteres in dieser Umgebung oft eingesetztes Material, jedoch ist es besser, darauf eine Patina aufzutragen, um ihm einen Anschein von Rustikalität zu verleihen. Für ein Bad im rustikalen Stil können restaurierte alte Elemente wie Holzbalken und -böden oder sogar Kiesel für die Verkleidung verwendet sowie antike Steintränken als Waschbecken angebracht werden. In zeitgenössischen, an den rustikalen Stil angelehnten Bädern werden heute sehr im Trend liegende Elemente mit groben und natürlichen Materialien kombiniert. Eine freistehende Badewanne wird zum Blickfang in einem klaren Raum mit sparsam eingesetzten Elementen und in dem verschiedene Naturmaterialien für Verkleidungen von Böden und Wänden verwendet werden. Die Schlichtheit der Formen und Kombination von Materialien charakterisieren diesen nahezu eklektisch konzipierten Bädertyp, der zugleich Rustikalität atmet. Der Stil wird von Farben und rauen Oberflächen geprägt: Stein- und Grautöne an Wänden, Badewannen und Mobiliar sorgen für eine antik traditionelle Note.

Salles de bains rustiques
Rustic Bathrooms

RUSTIKALE BADEZIMMER

Baños rústicos

Le style rustique traditionnel est celui utilisé pour définir le style de vie des maisons de campagne, celui qui retrace une forme de vie en contact direct avec la nature. La caractéristique principale de ce style de décoration est l'utilisation de matériaux naturels, simples et sans trop d'ornements pour le sol et les parois. Les carreaux de terracota et les dalles de marbre ancien sont des solutions idéales. Le marbre est d'une certaine froideur et convient au style classique bien qu'en choisissant un marbre ancien (particulièrement de couleur neutre et naturelle), on peut obtenir un effet contraire et donner un aspect chaleureux à une pièce. Le stucage des parois est un type de traitement fréquemment utilisé pour créer une ambiance campagnarde. Il offre un type de revêtement qui résiste bien à l'humidité et leur confère en même temps un aspect décoratif très naturel. Le stuc vient réalisé à base de plâtre et de pigments naturels comme l'oxyde, la terre cuite et on peut obtenir des revêtements réellement surprenants tels des parois peintes de couleurs qui présentent un aspect vieux et de grande personnalité. On peut combiner sans crainte les matériaux naturels dans une salle de bains rustique, bien que la majorité requièrent un traitement antérieur, leur permettant de supporter l'eau et l'humidité. Le bois est sans doute un autre matériel très employé pour ce type de pièce, bien que pour lui donner une allure rustique il est mieux de lui appliquer une vieille patine. Dans une salle de bains rustique, on peut employer des éléments antiques restaurés tels que de vieilles poutres, des parquets de bois et même des cailloux pour le revêtement, ainsi que des abreuvoirs de pierre en guise de lavabo. Les salles de bains actuelles ayant un air rustique, combinent des éléments qui sont très en vogue à des matériaux plus grossiers, rudimentaires et naturels. Une baignoire sur pieds (il y a des modèles actuels qui s'inspirent du passé) devient le protagoniste dans une pièce nette et sobre où divers types de revêtements naturels du sol et des parois viennent utilisés. La simplicité des formes et la combinaison des matériaux permettent de définir ce type de salles de bains quasi éclectiques tout en ayant un aspect d'inspiration rustique. Les couleurs et les textures rugueuses marquent aussi ce style: les tons de la pierre et les gris pour les parois, les baignoires et le mobilier leur confèrent une allure antique traditionnelle.

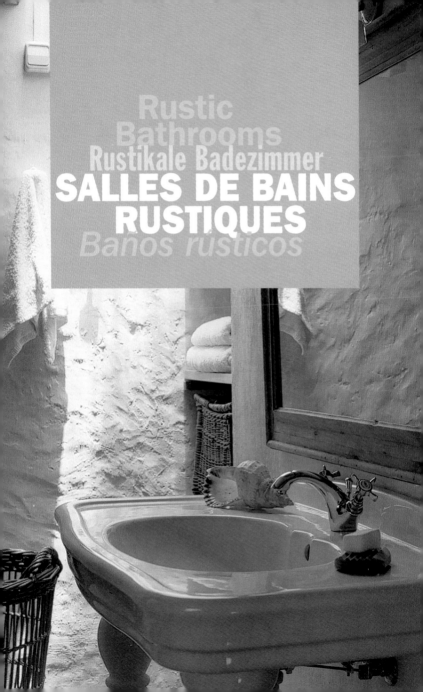

Rustic Bathrooms
Rustikale Badezimmer
SALLES DE BAINS RUSTIQUES
Baños rústicos

El estilo rústico tradicional es el que se utiliza para definir el estilo de vida de las casas de campo, las que recrean una forma de vivir en contacto directo con la naturaleza. La principal característica de este estilo decorativo es la utilización de materiales naturales, sencillos y sin demasiados ornamentos para suelos y paredes. Son ideales las baldosas de terracota o de barro cocido y las losetas de mármol envejecido. El mármol es un material que puede resultar frío y adecuado para estilos clásicos, aunque si se elige del tipo envejecido (especialmente de colores neutros y naturales), puede conseguirse el efecto contrario y añadir calidez al espacio. Los estucos de paredes son un tipo de tratamiento muy utilizado en ambientes campestres. Ofrecen un tipo de acabado que resiste muy bien la humedad y a la vez confiere un aspecto decorativo muy natural. El estuco se realiza con cal y pigmentos naturales como el óxido o la terracota y puede conseguir acabados realmente sorprendentes, como paredes pintadas de color que ofrecen un aspecto envejecido y de gran personalidad. Los materiales naturales pueden combinarse sin temor en un baño rústico, aunque la mayoría necesitan un tratamiento para soportar el agua y la humedad. La madera es, sin lugar a dudas, otro material muy utilizado en este tipo de espacios, aunque para darle un toque rústico es mejor aplicarle una pátina envejecida. En un baño rústico pueden utilizarse elementos antiguos recuperados como vigas y suelos de madera e incluso pueden colocarse cantos rodados para el revestimiento o antiguos bebederos de piedra como lavamanos. Los baños actuales con aire rústico combinan elementos que están muy en boga con materiales toscos y naturales. Una bañera con patas (hay modelos actuales inspirados en el pasado) adquiere protagonismo en un espacio limpio y sin demasiados elementos, que utiliza diversos tipos de revestimientos naturales para suelos y paredes. La simplicidad de formas y combinación de materiales permiten definir este tipo de baños en proyectos casi eclécticos pero con un toque de inspiración rústica. Los colores y las texturas rugosas marcan también este estilo: los tonos piedra y gris en paredes, bañeras y mobiliario, confieren un aire antiguo tradicional.

Salles de bains rustiques
Rustikale Badezimmer
BAÑOS RUSTICOS
Rustic Bathrooms

Goût rustique
Rustikaler Geschmack
RUSTIC TASTE
Sabor rústico

Architect: **Stéphane Bourgeois**

Thanks to the materials used, the concept of rustic style is updated with this bathroom. The originality stems from placing certain elements such as the bathtub, beside the bed, and from distributing other zones in a clearly differentiated space.

Die in diesem zum Schlafzimmer hin offenen Bad verwendeten Materialien stellen eine moderne Interpretation des rustikalen Stils dar. Die Originalität des Projekts entspringt der Idee, einige Elemente – wie z. B. die Badewanne – neben dem Bett zu platzieren und andere Bereiche in einem klar differenzierten Raum zu verteilen.

Les matériaux employés dans cette salle de bains qui est ouverte sur la chambre à coucher, actualisent le concepte de style rustique. L'originalité de ce projet est basée sur l'emplacement de certains éléments, comme par exemple, la baignoire qui se trouve à côté du lit, ainsi que de répartir les autres zones dans un espace clairement définit.

Los materiales empleados en este baño, abierto al dormitorio, actualizan el concepto de estilo rústico. La originalidad de este proyecto se basa en ubicar algunos elementos, como la bañera, al lado de la cama y distribuir otras zonas en un espacio claramente diferenciado.

Respect du passé
Reverenz an die Vergangenheit

RESPECT TO
THE PAST

Respeto al pasado

Architect: **Esperanza García Aubert**

Antiquité modernisé
Aktualisierte Antike
ACTUALIZED ANTIQUE
Antiguo actualizado

Photo © Montse Garriga

Rustique renové
Renovierter Landhausstil

RENOVATED RUSTIC

Rústico renovado

Inspiration naturelle
Natürliche Inspiration
NATURAL
INSPIRATION
Inspiración natural

Photo © José Luis Hausmann

Salles de bains modernes et avant-gardistes

Moderne und avantgardistische Badezimmer

MODERN AND AVANT-GARDE BATHROOMS

Baños actuales y vanguardistas

This section includes a wide variety of different projects. However, they share the common premise which is to place the bathroom at the forefront, and afford the opportunity to delight in creating very practical solutions. This style could almost be defined as ecclectic, since it resists categorizing based on past models, or contemporarily-defined conceptions. They represent an up-dating of the bathroom concept. The majority are original designs of expansive spaces, which open up to natural light and to the rest of the dwelling, and practically become the centerpiece of the home. The bathroom is no longer a hidden cubicle or room but rather, is open, comfortable and very practical and functional. It can even be used by more than one family member at a time, whilst still maintaining its privacy. Here, bathrooms designed for the new industrial loft style and designs where one unique room is reserved for the bath, are included in this style. What they have in common is that there is a delimited space for each of the bathroom needs, based on a wise ordering of the elements, and a polished image. Different materials that complement each other are combined: wood, glass, steel and synthetic materials. The attempt is to achieve very original lines with simple, yet very daring shapes. Some projects, which make use of very elegant materials and decorative details, are reminiscent of a classical style, though they are more than duly up-dated. Others, spring from more vanguard approaches. Here, we can find very contemporary toilets, bathtubs, and showers, and original-style hand basins. New materials for coverings are being used: plastics which are very durable and are great insulators, laminates which are very decorative and afford a wide variety of finishes, metals which are extremely resistant to cuts, nicks and water, and wood derivatives such as linoleum and cork which are nearly waterproof, and lastly, natural materials like stone. Polished natural stone can be smooth and afford easy cleaning.

Salles de bains modernes et avant-gardistes
Moderne und avantgardistische Badezimmer
MODERN AND AVANT-GARDE BATHROOMS
Baños actuales y vanguardistas

In diesem Kapitel wird eine große Anzahl unterschiedlicher Projekte zusammengefasst, die eines gemeinsam haben: Das Bad als elementaren Raum zum Entspannen, in dem zugleich praktische Lösungen angewandt werden. Der für diese Räume charakteristische Stil kann als geradezu eklektisch bezeichnet werden, denn er vermeidet bewusst jegliche Klassifizierung, die durch ein vergangenes oder derzeit bestimmendes modernes Design inspiriert ist. Es handelt sich dabei um originelle Vorschläge – meist für große Räume mit natürlicher Lichtquelle –, die unsere Vorstellung vom Badezimmer verändern. Dieses öffnet sich dem Licht und dem Rest des Hauses und wird zu einem Raum von herausragender Bedeutung. Das Bad ist nicht länger ein versteckter Raum, sondern offen, bequem, sehr praktisch und funktional, denn es kann zur gleichen Zeit von mehr als einem Familienmitglied benutzt werden, ohne dass dadurch die nötige Privatsphäre verletzt würde. Zu dieser Stilrichtung zählen die im Rahmen des neuen Loft-Designs entworfenen Bäder sowie einige Projekte, die einen einzelnen Raum für das Badezimmer vorsehen. Übereinstimmung herrscht bei ihnen dahingehend, dass einer jeden Tätigkeit ein Raum zugewiesen wird, wobei die verschiedenen Elemente intelligent angeordnet werden und Wert auf das äußere Erscheinungsbild gelegt wird. Dabei kommt es zu Kombinationen sehr unterschiedlicher Materialien: Holz, Glas, Stahl sowie synthetische Materialien, die einander ergänzen, und man setzt auf Elemente mit ganz originellen Linien und nüchternen Formen, die durchaus gewagt sind. Einige Projekte scheinen an einen klassischen Stil angelehnt zu sein – obgleich in höchstem Maße modernisiert – und verwenden sehr elegante Materialien sowie dekorative Details. Andere scheinen sich eher an avantgardistischen Trends zu orientieren, mit hochmodernen Toiletten, Badewannen und Duschen sowie Waschbecken mit originellen Linien. Neue Beschichtungen werden verwendet wie Kunststoffe (von außerordentlicher Härte und stark isolierend), Laminate (sehr dekorativ und mit vielfältigen Oberflächen), Metallverkleidungen (mit hoher Widerstandsfähigkeit gegen mechanische Einwirkungen und Wasser) und auf Holz basierende Stoffe wie Linoleum und Kork (nahezu undurchlässig) sowie Naturmaterialien wie Stein. Polierter Naturstein bietet glatte Oberflächen und ist leicht zu reinigen.

Salles de bains modernes et avant-gardistes
Modern and Avant-garde Bathrooms

MODERNE UND AVANTGARDISTISCHE BADEZIMMER

Baños actuales y vanguardistas

Cette catégorie englobe une variété de projets différents, ayant tous pour but de donner à la salle de bains le rôle principal; un endroit qu'on apprécie, avec des solutions très pratiques. Le style définissant cet endroit est quasi éclectique et tente d'échapper à une classification inspirée du passé ou d'une idée actuelle définie. Il s'agit d'options originales, en majorité de grands espaces ouverts à la lumière naturelle, qui actualisent la conception de la salle de bains. Celle-ci s'ouvre à la lumière et au reste de la maison et se transforme quasiment en protagoniste. La salle de bains n'est plus une pièce cachée, mais ouverte, confortable, très pratique et fonctionnelle, pouvant être utilisée en même temps par plusieurs membres de la famille, sans pour autant perdre l'intimité requise. Dans cette catégorie on trouve également les salles de bains créent dans le concept du loft ainsi que certains projets qui ne prévoient qu'une seule pièce : la salle de bains. Ce qu'elles ont en commun étant un espace délimité pour les différents besoins comprenant un sage ordonnance des éléments et une image soignée. On combine des matériaux très différents: du bois, du verre, de l'acier, des matériaux synthétiques. Ils se complètent et misent sur des lignes originales, de formes sobres et très audacieuses. Certains projets rappellent un style classique très actualisé. Ils emploient des matériaux et des détails décoratifs très élégants. D'autres s'inspirent de tendances avant-gardistes avec des sanitaires, des baignoires, et des douches très modernes, des lavabos ayant des lignes originales et des revêtements nouveaux tels que le plastique (qui est résistant et isole très bien), les laminés (très décoratifs et offrant une grande variétés de finitions possibles), le métal (très résistant aux coup et à l'eau), et tous les dérivés du bois comme le linoléum et le liège (pratiquement imperméable), et enfin des matériaux naturels comme la pierre. La pierre naturelle polie a une surface lisse et facile à nettoyer.

Modern and Avant-garde Bathrooms

Moderne und avantgardistische Badezimmer

SALLES DE BAINS MODERNES ET AVANT-GARDISTES

Baños actuales y vanguardistas

En este apartado se engloba gran variedad de proyectos diferentes marcados por la necesidad de convertir el baño en protagonista; es un espacio para disfrutar en donde se crean soluciones muy prácticas. El estilo que define estos espacios es casi ecléctico, puesto que intenta huir de catalogaciones inspiradas en un pasado o en una concepción actual definida. Se trata de opciones originales, mayoritariamente de grandes espacios abiertos a la luz natural, que actualizan el concepto del baño. Este se abre a la luz y al resto de la casa y se transforma en un espacio casi protagonista. El cuarto de baño ya no es una habitación escondida, sino abierta, cómoda y muy práctica y funcional, puesto que puede ser utilizada al mismo tiempo por más de un miembro de la familia sin por ello perder la intimidad necesaria. En este estilo pueden incluirse los baños proyectados bajo el nuevo concepto industrial de loft y también algunos proyectos que reservan una única habitación para el baño. Todos coinciden en reservar un espacio para cada una de las tareas, incorporando una sabia ordenación de los elementos y una cuidada imagen. Se combinan materiales muy diferentes —madera, cristal, acero, materiales sintéticos...— que se complementan, y se apuesta por elementos de líneas muy originales, de formas sobrias y muy atrevidas. Algunos proyectos parecen recordar un estilo clásico aunque sobradamente actualizado, e incluyen elegantes materiales y detalles que lo decoran. Otros quizá se inspiren en las tendencias más vanguardistas, con sanitarios, bañeras y duchas muy actuales, lavamanos de líneas originales y nuevos revestimientos, como los plásticos (de extraordinaria dureza y gran aislamiento), los laminados (muy decorativos y con múltiples acabados), los revestimientos metálicos (de elevada resistencia a los golpes y al agua) y los derivados de la madera, como el linóleo y el corcho (prácticamente impermeables), además de los materiales naturales como la piedra. La piedra natural pulimentada, por ejemplo, evita la rugosidad y es fácil de limpiar.

Salles de bains
modernes et
avant-gardistes

Moderne und
avantgardistische Badezimmer

BAÑOS ACTUALES
Y VANGUARDISTAS

Modern and
Avant-garde
Bathrooms

Ecléctique actuelle
Zeitgenössischer Eklektizismus
CONTEMPORARY
ECLECTIC
Architect: **Blockarchitecture**

Ecléctico actual

Jeux géometriques
Geometrische Spiele
GEOMETRIC GAMES
Juegos geométricos

Architect: **Johnson Chou**

Ambiance ouverte
Offenes Ambiente
OPEN AMBIENCE
Ambiente abierto

Profondeur immense
Grenzenlose Tiefe
SPACIOUS VOLUME
Inmensa profundidad

Architect: **Stephen Varady Architecture**

Espace translucide
Transparenter Raum
TRANSLUCENT SPACE
Espacio translúcido

Interiorists: **Nancy Robbins, Lluís Victori**

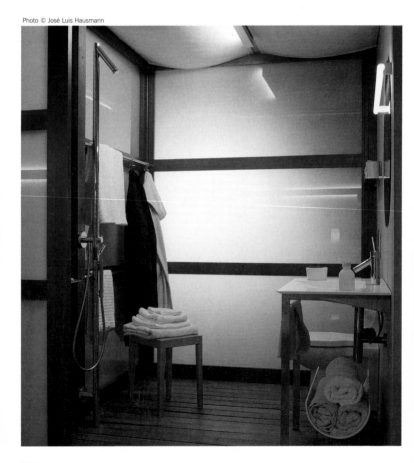

Sans coins
Ohne Ecken
NO CORNERS
Sin esquinas

Architect: **Holger Kleine**

Formes pures
Reine Formen
PURITY OF FORMS
Pureza de formas

Architect: **Holger Kleine**

Photo © Werner Huthmacher

Noir et jaune
Schwarz und Gelb
BLACK AND YELLOW
Negro y amarillo

Architect: **Jennifer Randall & Associates**

Vert pomme
Apfelgrün
APPLE GREEN
Verde manzana

Photo © Jordi Miralles

Ouvert à la relaxation
Offen für Entspannung
OPEN TO RELAX
Abierto al descanso

Photo © Jordi Miralles

231

Lignes verticales
Vertikale Linien
Architect: **Hüffer Ramin**
VERTICAL LINES
Líneas verticales

Le grand bleu
Das grosse Blau
THE BIG BLUE
El gran azul

Architects: **Kalhöfer-Korschildgen**

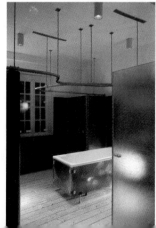

A folding screen serves to structure the space in this rehabilitation. The new elements cover the original structure. New flexible spaces can be created with the removable curtains.

Bei einem Badeinbau wird ein Paravent als räumlich ordnendes Element eingesetzt. Der Einbau überlagert die alte Struktur. Mit Hilfe von Vorhängen können neue flexible Bereiche im Raum geschaffen werden.

Lors de la construction d'une salle de bains on peut utiliser un paravent pour ordonner la pièce. En l'installant au plafond à la facon d'un rideaux que l'on peut tirer, qui crée des espaces distincts mais très fluides à l'intérieur même de la pièce.

Un biombo sirve como instrumento para estructurar el espacio en esta rehabilitación. Los nuevos elementos tapan la estructura original; con las cortinas extraíbles se pueden crear espacios maleables.

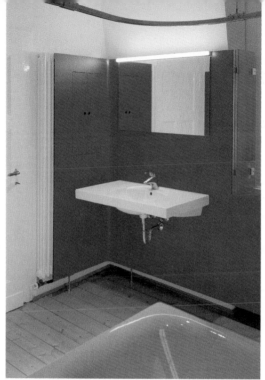

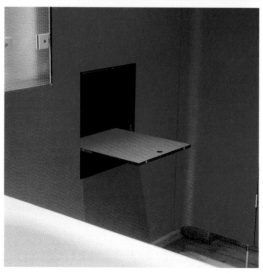

243

Salles de bains minimalistes

Minimalistische Badezimmer

MINIMALISTIC BATHROOMS

Baños minimalistas

What bathrooms grouped together in this category have in common is that, space and light take center stage. Often we are not dealing with rooms with reduced dimensions with an imperious need to maximize the use of the available space, but rather, we are dealing with large bathrooms designed with a minimum of furniture, so as to achieve a clean uncluttered space without ornaments. The elements are chosen mainly because of their practicality and because of the nature of the materials: small hand basins made of natural stone, fixtures built into the walls, hanging toilets and niches for stowing objects in. Bathrooms of Zen aesthetics are included here; immaculately white or dark but with few elements, only what is strictly needed. The bathroom as a place of rest and relaxation is given precedence over other concerns, thus the wet zones acquire more importance that the others. Although there is no strict rule, minimalist bathrooms tend to be open spaces without walls or partition screens to separate elements. Instead, an intelligent distribution allows each zone to be clearly delimited. Thus, they take maximum advantage of natural light, or the bathroom is integrated into the bedroom in an almost natural way. This is a new life-style akin to those of lofts where spaces are not permanent but rather, are interchangeable and adaptable to the particular moment. The nature of a bathroom necessitates greater planning as there is a permanent water installation. Nonetheless, this is not a drawback to it being an open space (while at the same time, allowing for privacy to be maintained). The materials employed for this type of bathroom are both natural and durable: dark woods such as iroko or wenge, natural stone, concrete which is very much in vogue now, and a construction material consisting of a cement, conglomerate and sand which can be tinted with natural pigments to achieve a very original finish, so very suitable in modern ambiences. The key to these spaces is in the aesthetics where we find carefully chosen clean shapes, almost infinite and comfortable spaces, spaces without furniture and with few complements. It is a minimal space to be enjoyed in half-empty surroundings, which are very special.

MINIMALISTIC
BATHROOMS

Salles de bains
minimalistes
Minimalistische
Badezimmer
*Baños
minimalistas*

Bei den unter dieser Stilrichtung zusammengefassten Bädern kommen Raum und Licht die größte Bedeutung zu. In vielen Fällen handelt es sich dabei nicht um kleine Räume, bei denen man alle Möglichkeiten zur Ausschöpfung des vorhandenen Platzes nutzen muss, sondern um weiträumige Bäder, die mit einem Minimum an Mobiliar ausgestattet sind, um einen klaren, schmucklosen Raum zu schaffen. Die hier verwendeten Elemente werden in erster Linie aus praktischen Erwägungen und aufgrund der Beschaffenheit der Materialien ausgewählt: kleine Waschbecken aus Naturstein, Unterputzarmaturen, Wand-WCs, für Aufbewahrungszwecke genutzte Nischen. Auch die Bäder im Zen-Stil sind in diesem Kapitel enthalten: tadellos weiße oder dunkle Bäder mit wenigen und nur den notwendigsten Elementen. Priorität in diesen Badezimmern genießen Ruhe und Entspannung, weswegen der Nassbereich bzw. die Badewanne mehr in den Mittelpunkt rücken als die übrigen Teile des Raums. Zwar gibt es keine festgeschriebene Norm, doch sind minimalistische Bäder in der Regel offene Räume ohne Wände oder Mauern, welche die Elemente trennen würden: Die einzelnen Teile werden lediglich durch eine wohl durchdachte Anordnung definiert. So gelingt eine optimale Ausnutzung des Tageslichts, oder das Bad wird auf fast natürliche Art und Weise in ein Schlafzimmer integriert. Es handelt sich hierbei um eine neue Wohnform, die mit den heutigen Lofts verwandt ist, in denen Räume nicht fixiert, sondern austauschbar sind, weil sie sich an die Bedürfnisse des Augenblicks anpassen. Die Natur des Badezimmers erfordert eine spezifischere Planung, da eine feste Wasserinstallation notwendig ist, wenngleich dies durchaus mit dem Konzept des offenen Raumes vereinbar ist (und ohne dass dies zu einer Verletzung der nötigen Privatsphäre führen würde). Die verwendeten Materialien sind sowohl natürlich als auch widerstandsfähig: dunkle Hölzer wie Iroko oder Wengue, Naturstein und der heute sehr populäre Beton – ein Baustoff aus Zement, Kalkgemenge und Sand, der besonders für moderne Umgebungen geeignet ist und mit Naturpigmenten gefärbt werden kann, um eine originale Oberfläche zu erhalten. Das Geheimnis dieser Räume liegt in ihrer ästhetischen Ausstrahlung: ausgewogene, klare Formen, beinahe endlose und komfortable Räume ohne Mobiliar und fast bar jeder Ausstattung. Ein minimaler Raum der durch seine karge, wenn auch ganz besondere Umgebung wirkt.

Salles de bains
minimalistes
Minimalistic
Bathrooms

MINIMALISTISCHE
BADEZIMMER

*Baños
minimalistas*

Les salles de bains conçues dans ce style donnent le rôle le plus important à l'espace et à la lumière. Dans beaucoup de cas, il ne s'agit pas de petites pièces nécessitant des ressources particulières pour exploiter la surface existante, mais de grandes salles de bains ayant un minimum de mobilier pour obtenir un espace pur et sans ornements. Les éléments incorporés sont choisis principalement pour leur aspect pratique et pour leur matériaux naturels : petits lavabos de pierre naturelle, robinetterie encastrée dans la parois, sanitaires suspendus, niches utilisées pour ranger divers objets. Les salles de bains de style zen sont comprises dans cette catégorie : d'un blanc immaculé ou très foncées, mais avec peut d'éléments, uniquement ceux qui sont nécessaires. Ces salles de bains donnent la priorité au repos et à la relaxation, et la zone d'eau joue un rôle plus important que les autres parties de la pièce. Bien qu'il n'existe pas de norme fixe, les salles de bains minimalistes tendent à être des espaces ouverts, sans parois ou murets de séparation. Seule une répartition intelligente permet de délimiter clairement chacune des zones. Ainsi elles profitent au maximum de la lumière du jour, ou sont intégrées de façon naturelle à la chambre à coucher. Il s'agit d'un nouveau style de vivre apparenté a celui des lofts où les espaces ne sont pas fixes mais plutôt interchangeables et pouvant être adaptés aux besoins du moment. La salle de bains nécessite une planification importante due au fait que l'installation de la tuyauterie est fixe, bien que cet aspect ne l'empêche pas d'être un espace ouvert (tout en gardant l'intimité nécessaire). Les matériaux employés pour ce type de salles de bains sont naturels et résistants à la fois : Les bois foncés tels que l'iroco et le wengué, les pierres naturelles de même que le béton, qui est très en vogue en ce moment, et un matériel de construction constitué de ciment, de conglomérat et de sable qui peut être teinté avec des pigments naturels, donnent un résultat très original et qui convient bien à une ambiance moderne. Le secret de ces espaces est leur esthétique : des formes soignées et nettes, des espaces infinis et confortables, sans mobilier ni accessoires. Un espace minimal à apprécier dans un environnement à moitié dénudé, bien que très spécial.

Minimalistic
Bathrooms
Minimalistische
Badezimmer
SALLES DE BAINS
MINIMALISTES
Baños
minimalistas

Los baños que se incluyen en este estilo coinciden en dar el mayor protagonismo al espacio y a la luz. En muchos casos no se trata de estancias pequeñas que requieran recursos para aprovechar los metros, sino de baños amplios que buscan el mínimo mobiliario para conseguir un espacio limpio y sin ornamentos. Los elementos que se incorporan se eligen principalmente por su aspecto práctico y por la naturaleza de sus materiales: lavamanos mínimos de piedra natural, griferías empotradas en las paredes, sanitarios suspendidos, hornacinas que se utilizan para guardar enseres. Los baños de estética zen se incluyen en este apartado: baños inmaculadamente blancos u oscuros pero con pocos elementos, apenas los imprescindibles. Estos baños dan prioridad al descanso y a la relajación, de ahí que la zona de aguas adquiera más protagonismo que las otras partes de la estancia. Aunque no existe ninguna norma fija, los baños minimalistas suelen ser espacios abiertos, sin paredes ni muretes que separen los elementos: sólo una pensada distribución zonifica cada parte. Así se aprovecha la luz natural al máximo o se integra el baño casi de una forma natural en un dormitorio. Se trata de una nueva forma de vivir que guarda relación con los actuales lofts, donde los espacios no son fijos y sí intercambiables, puesto que se adaptan a las necesidades del momento. La naturaleza del cuarto de baño precisa una mayor planificación, al necesitar una instalación de agua fija, pero este aspecto no impide que sea un espacio abierto (sin que esto signifique perder la intimidad necesaria). Los materiales empleados para este tipo de baño son naturales y resistentes a la vez: maderas oscuras como el iroco o el wengue, piedras naturales e incluso materiales muy en boga como el hormigón, un soporte constructivo compuesto por cemento, conglomerado y arena, muy adecuado en ambientes modernos, que puede teñirse con pigmentos naturales y conseguir un acabado muy original. El secreto de estos espacios está en su estética: formas cuidadas y limpias, espacios casi infinitos y cómodos, sin mobiliario ni casi complementos. Un espacio minimalista para disfrutar en un entorno semidesnudo pero muy especial.

Salles de bains minimalistes
Minimalistische Badezimmer
BAÑOS MINIMALISTAS
Minimalistic Bathrooms

Simplicité japonaise
Japanische Schlichtheit

JAPANESE SIMPLICITY

Architect: **Kenji Hashimoto**

Simplicidad japonesa

Sans murs
Ohne Wände
WITHOUT WALLS
Sin paredes

Architect: **Shigeru Ban**

Minimal style defines this original project. The vast space is distributed exclusively by means of the elements that make it up, as there is an absence of walls and partitions. Light flows in a natural way in this bathroom, which is opened out to the environment.

Dieses originelle Projekt wird vom Minimalen geprägt. Die Aufteilung des großen Raumes erfolgt ausschließlich durch die Elemente, die er enthält – ohne Wände oder Trennwände. Das Licht strömt auf natürliche Weise durch das gesamte, zur Umgebung hin geöffnete Bad.

Un style minimal définit ce projet original. La répartition, à l'intérieur de ce grand espace, se fait uniquement au moyen des éléments qu'il contient, sans murs ni parois de séparation. La lumière peut se déplacer de façon naturelle dans cette salle de bains ouverte sur le paysage.

El estilo minimal define este original proyecto. El gran espacio se distribuye únicamente a través de los elementos que lo integran, sin paredes ni muros divisorios. La luz circula de forma natural por todo este baño, abierto al paisaje.

Essence orientale
Orientalische Essenz
ORIENTAL ESSENCE
Esencia oriental

Architect: **Ayhan Ozan**

Photo © Bjorg Photography

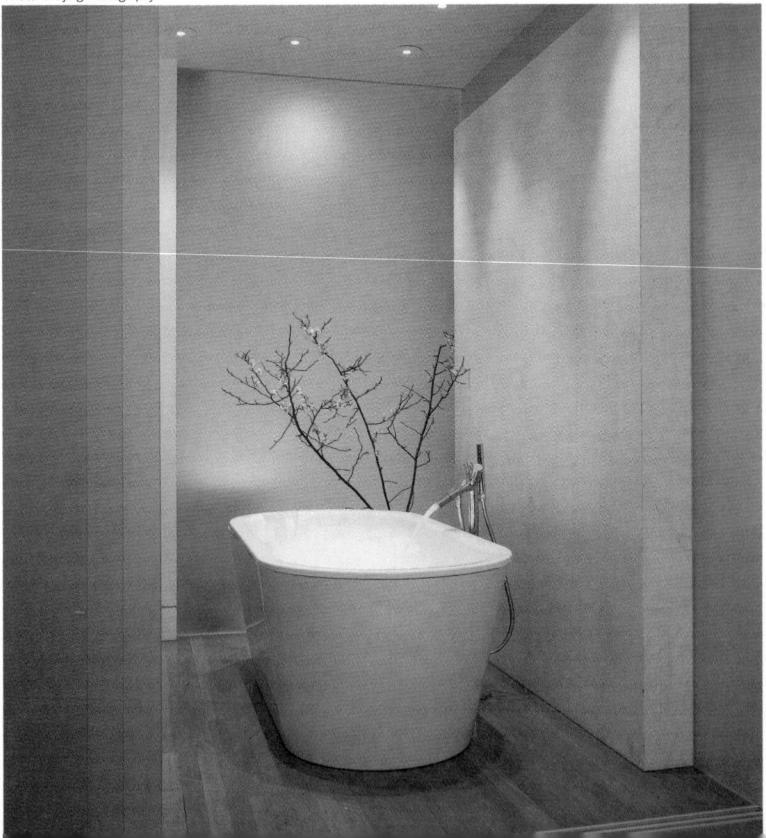

Formes simples
Einfache Formen
SIMPLE FORMS
Formas simples

Photo © Joshua Mc Hugh

Culture Zen
Zen Kultur
ZEN CULTURE
Cultura zen

Photo © José Luis Hausmann

Minimum originale
Minimalistisches Original
MINIMAL
ORIGINAL
Architect: **Lynx Architecture**

Un mínimo original

Photo © Andreas J. Focke

Cabine en fer
Eisenkabine
IRON CABIN
Architects: **Grollmitz-Zappe**
Cabina de acero

**Bains
publiques**
Öffentliche Badezimmer
PUBLIC
BATHROOMS
Baños públicos

Generally speaking, public baths tend to be characterized by a very modernday style. Designed to be clean, practical and very functional, they are usually placed in a restaurant, hotel or gymnasium. Many tendencies opt for an ecclectic syle, as the visitors and users will have very varied and differentiated tastes, although the most recent creations exhibit very original designs. Whatever the style, it is interesting to observe the solutions for dividing the space into the corresponding zones for the bathroom fixtures, showers and the dressing area. These types of baths require extensive spaces with an intelligent distribution, which afford a clear delimitation for each of the zones in such a way that, privacy is maintained whilst not becoming too isolated. To delimit each of the services, especially the shower and toilet, it is not advisable to employ open or diaphanous solutions such as half-height walls or glass screens, as it is imperative to maintain privacy. Using the same materials throughout the design, but with different colors, can provide splendid results. Dual-tone (blue and yellow) stoneware or ceramic tiles for instance, may be used to clearly differentiate two zones, while uniting them in the same space. Similarly, diverse materials can be brought together, by utilizing tones which are akin (gray, black ...). It is essential to provide proper artificial illumination in this type of baths, as each zone must have its own lighting. Of equal importance is the choice of washbasins and bathroom fittings, which may be of simple design, but functional. Likewise, the fixtures will add a touch of distinction or elegance, depending on the model chosen. Lastly, the presence of mirrors is indispensable. As a general rule, this type of installation, unless it be a gymnasium, does not require an excessive amount of furniture, as a spacious distribution which facilitates the free circulation of light and the users, is what is essential.

Bains
publiques
Öffentliche Badezimmer
PUBLIC
BATHROOMS
Baños públicos

Im Allgemeinen werden öffentliche Bäder eindeutig von zeitgenössischen Trends geprägt. Sie sind in Restaurants, Hotels oder Fitnesscentern zu finden und ihre wichtigste Funktion besteht im Anbieten eines praktischen, peinlich sauberen und sehr funktionellen Raums. Einige Trends setzen auf einen eklektischen Stil, da die Personen, welche die Bäder aufsuchen, einen ganz unterschiedlichen Geschmack haben können, wenngleich die jüngsten Einrichtungen äußerst originellen Umgebungen den Vorzug geben. Unabhängig von der jeweiligen Stilrichtung ist es interessant zu beobachten, mit welchen Mitteln die Aufteilung eines jeden Raums erfolgt – ungeachtet dessen, ob es sich um die Bereiche von WCs, Duschen oder Waschtischen handelt. Diese Art von Bädern erfordert große Räume mit einer intelligenten Verteilung, sodass eine klare Trennung zwischen den einzelnen Bereichen erfolgen kann, um ein Höchstmaß an Privatsphäre zu gewährleisten, ohne dabei die Elemente voneinander zu isolieren. Bei der Abgrenzung der einzelnen Kabinen (dies gilt insbesondere für Duschen und WCs) ist von offenen oder transparenten Lösungen wie halbhohen Mauern oder Glastrennwänden abzuraten, denn die Intimität ist strikt zu wahren. Die Verwendung derselben Materialien im gesamten Raum bei unterschiedlicher Farbgestaltung kann ein guter Weg sein, um ein attraktives Gesamtbild zu schaffen. Keramikfliesen in zwei Farbtönen (Blau und Gelb) z. B. können zwei Zonen deutlich optisch unterscheiden und sie gleichzeitig in einem Raum vereinen, oder es werden verschiedene Materialien in ähnlichen Farbtönen (Schwarz, Grau, ...) verwendet, wodurch eine Verbindung zwischen allen Elementen hergestellt wird. Eine korrekte künstliche Beleuchtung ist in dieser Art Bäder von grundlegender Bedeutung, weil es notwendig ist, Licht in jeden der Bereiche zu bringen. Nicht weniger wichtig ist die Auswahl der Waschbecken und WCs (die bei hoher Funktionalität durchaus schlicht sein können) sowie der Armaturen (die – je nach Modell – für einen Hauch von Gediegenheit oder Eleganz sorgen) und des gänzlich unverzichtbaren Spiegels. In der Regel erfordert diese Art von Bädern – sofern es sich nicht um ein Fitnesscenter handelt – kein vollständiges Mobiliar, denn im Mittelpunkt steht hier eine großzügige Raumverteilung zugunsten des freien Durchgangs von Licht und Benutzern.

Bains
publiques
Public Bathrooms
ÖFFENTLICHE
BADEZIMMER
Baños públicos

De nos jours les bains publiques sont à nouveau très en vogue. Ils se trouvent dans les restaurants, les hôtels ou centres de fitness, et ont comme fonction principale de se convertir en un espace pratique, soigné et très fonctionnel. Certaines tendances misent sur un style éclectique, les personnes qui y viennent ayant de goûts très différents, bien que pour les nouvelles créations on préfèrent un cadre extrêmement original. Le style étant ce qu'il est, il est intéressant d'observer les solutions employées pour différencier chacun des espaces, que ce soit pour la division des sanitaires, des douches ou la zone des tables de toilette. Ce type de bains requière de grands espaces ayant une répartition intelligente qui permet d'établir une séparation claire entre chacune des parties pour respecter au maximum le côté privé sans en faire des éléments mis à l'écart. Pour délimiter chacun de ces services, (en particulier les douches et les sanitaires), il n'est pas conseillé d'utiliser des solutions ouvertes ou transparentes, tels que des murs à mi-hauteur ou des paravents en verre afin de preserver à tout prix l'intimité. Les utilisations des mêmes matériaux dans tous les espaces, en employant des couleurs différentes, peut donner un résultat très attrayant. De la mosaïque ou des carreaux de deux couleurs (bleus et jaunes), par exemple, peuvent différencier clairement les zones tout en ayant une unité dans l'espace ; l'autre possibilité étant d'utiliser des matériaux différents ayant un ton similaire (noir, gris …) cela menant à unir tous les éléments. Un bon éclairage artificiel est fondamental dans ce type de bains. Il est nécessaire de doter chacune des zones de sa propre lumière. Le choix des lavabos et des sanitaires n'étant pas moins important (ils peuvent avoir des lignes simples et être très fonctionnels), de même que la robinetterie, qui ajoutera une touche de distinction ou d'élégance suivant le modèle choisi, et des miroirs qui sont absolument indispensables. En général, à moins qu'il ne s'agisse centre de sport, un mobilier complet n'est pas nécessaire l'essentiel étant la répartition de l'espace, permettant la libre circulation de la lumière et des usagers.

Public
Bathrooms
Öffentliche Badezimmer
BAINS
PUBLIQUES
Baños públicos

Por norma general, los baños públicos son de marcadas tendencias actuales. Ubicados en un restaurante, un hotel o un gimnasio, su principal función es convertirse en un espacio práctico, pulcro y muy funcional. Algunas tendencias apuestan por un estilo ecléctico, puesto que las personas que los visitan pueden tener gustos muy diferenciados, aunque los de nueva creación prefieren proyectar entornos sumamente originales. Sea cual sea su estilo, es interesante observar las soluciones creadas para distribuir cada uno de los espacios, ya sea en la división de sanitarios, duchas o en la zona del tocador. Este tipo de baños necesita grandes espacios con una organización inteligente que permita establecer una clara separación entre cada una de las partes, de modo que respeten al máximo la privacidad, pero que a la vez no se conviertan en elementos aislados. Para delimitar cada uno de los servicios (en especial las duchas y los sanitarios), no es aconsejable utilizar soluciones abiertas o diáfanas, como muros a media altura o mamparas de cristal, puesto que debe preservarse la intimidad con rigurosidad. La utilización de los mismos materiales en todo el espacio empleando diferentes colores puede ser una buena solución para conseguir un atractivo resultado final. Gresite o azulejos cerámicos en dos tonos (azul y amarillo), por ejemplo, pueden diferenciar claramente dos zonas y unirlas en un mismo espacio, o bien utilizar diversos materiales de tonos similares (negro, gris...), ya que consiguen aunar todos los elementos. Una correcta iluminación artificial es fundamental en este tipo de baños, puesto que es necesario dotar de luz propia cada una de las divisiones. No menos importante es la elección de los lavamanos y sanitarios (que pueden ser de líneas simples aunque muy funcionales), así como las griferías, (que añadirán un toque de distinción o de elegancia, en función del modelo elegido) y el espejo, totalmente imprescindible. Por norma general, a menos que se trate de un gimnasio, este tipo de baños no rprecisan un completo mobiliario, puesto que lo esencial es una distribución espaciosa que apueste por la libre circulación de la luz y de los usuarios.

Bains publiques
Öffentliche Badezimmer
BAÑOS PÚBLICOS
Public Bathrooms

Zones particulières
Einzelne Zonen
PARTICULAR ZONES
Zonas particulares

Photo © Lluís Miras

Stoneware is what unifies, and at the same time, differentiates, all of the zones of this public bath. The color yellow identifies the toilet zone whereas the same material, but in blue, denotes the dressing and washbasin area.

Die Keramikfliesen stellen das einende Element für alle Bereiche dieses öffentlichen Bades dar und dienen zugleich zur Differenzierung der einzelnen Bereiche.
Die Verkleidung in Gelb kennzeichnet die Kabinen für die WCs, während das gleiche Material in Blau den Bereich für Waschtisch und Waschbecken definiert.

La mosaïque unit les différentes zones de ces bains publiques et sert en même temps à les différencier. Le revêtement jaune identifie la partie dédiée aux sanitaires tandis que le même matériel en bleu définit la partie des tables de toilette et des lavabos.

El gresite unifica todas las zonas de este baño público y sirve a la vez para diferenciar cada zona. El revestimiento en amarillo identifica los compartimentos dedicados a los sanitarios, mientras que el mismo material en azul define la zona del tocador y los lavamanos.

Combinaison élégante
Elegante Kombination
ELEGANT COMBINATION
Combinación elegante

Photo © Lluís Miras

290

Brillant et platre
Glänzend und Silber
SHINY AND SILVER
Brillo y plata

Photo © Lluís Miras

295

Ordre moderne
Moderne Ordnung
MODERN ORDER
Orden moderno

297

Salles de bains pour espaces réduits

Badezimmer in kleinen Räumen

BATHROOMS IN SMALL PLACES

Baños en espacios pequeños

In spite of the fact that few square meters are at your disposal, a lovely and practical bathroom can still be designed. Nowadays, we find very well designed rooms with very intelligent use of available resources, that make maximum use of available space. Thanks to the clever use of a few tricks, they are able to make a bathroom appear much larger. Simplicity of lines and the minimum use of furniture, which permits everything to be stowed away, are required, when a bath is small. Functionality is of utmost importance here, as all useful and necessary elements, must be placed in a minimum of space. The first rule of thumb is to add luminosity. To do this, a large window to the exterior may be opened, or glass blocks can be employed, so as to obtain light from the other rooms. Since we cannot always resort to the aforementioned, other options may be a large mirror placed over the washbasin, or other smaller mirrors strategically situated. Mirrors multiply light and may even be able to make a space appear larger (as long as their use is not excessive). The colors for the walls and floor must be judiciously chosen. Light colors such as whites, light natural tones and even yellows (which are very luminous), make a room seem larger. Therefore, they are ideal for rooms of limited dimensions. On the other hand, though darker colors confer personality to a room, they deprive it of light. If we opt for wall or floor coverings, it is best to keep them small and the tones should be very light. If, despite this, we still wish to install dark wood, it should be combined with luminous and light elements. In small bathrooms we can make use of toilets hanging from the wall, and minimum-size fixtures. Likewise, we may use a minimum of functional furniture such as a washbasin built in or recessed into the wall and held up by light metal legs, or small corner cabinets or shelves, or built-in cabinets. In small spaces it is best to forget about the bidet and just put in the toilet, as well as replacing the bathtub with a shower and changing the traditional sink on a pedestal for one built into, or backing onto, a wall. If storage space is needed, a low cabinet under the counter may be added. Light materials such as glass and metal are very suitable for small spaces.

Salles de bains
pour espaces réduits
Badezimmer in
kleinen Räumen

BATHROOMS IN
SMALL PLACES

*Baños en espacios
pequeños*

Auch wenn nur wenig Fläche zur Verfügung steht, muss man auf ein schönes und praktisches Badezimmer nicht verzichten. Es gibt heutzutage Räume, die sich durch einen sehr ausgeklügelten und äußerst intelligenten Einsatz der verfügbaren Möglichkeiten auszeichnen, die den zur Verfügung stehenden Platz optimal nutzen, während ein paar gleichzeitig angewandte kleine Tricks den Raum größer wirken lassen. Ein Bad von kleinen Dimensionen erfordert einfache Linien sowie eine Beschränkung des Mobiliars auf ein Minimum, in dem alles Notwendige verstaut werden kann. Bei diesem Bädertyp ist der funktionale Aspekt von großer Bedeutung, denn das Wichtigste ist hier, alle nützlichen Elemente auf eingeschränktem Raum unterzubringen. Die Regel Nummer eins lautet: mehr Helligkeit. Einige Konzepte setzen auf große Außenfenster oder verwenden Glasziegel, um vom Licht benachbarter Räume zu profitieren. Man kann jedoch nicht immer auf diese Lösungen zurückgreifen. Dann ist es geschickt, mit einem großen Spiegel über dem Waschbecken oder mehreren kleinen Spiegeln zu arbeiten, da diese das Licht vielfach zurückwerfen und so einen Raum optisch vergrößern. Ein weiterer Faktor, der Beachtung verdient, ist die für Wände und Böden verwendete Farbe. Helle Farbtöne lassen einen Raum größer erscheinen: Weiß-, Creme- und selbst (sehr helle) Gelbtöne sind bestens für kleine Räume geeignet, während dunklere Farben – wenngleich sie ihnen viel Persönlichkeit verleihen – das Licht nehmen. Hinsichtlich der Verkleidung empfiehlt es sich, kleine Teile in sehr hellen Farbtönen zu verwenden. Wenn man trotzdem z. B. dunkles Holz im Bad einsetzen möchte, ist es besser, dieses mit hellen und strahlenden Elementen zu kombinieren. Sanitäranlagen sollten in kleinen Bädern an die Wand gehängt werden. Des Weiteren sollte darauf geachtet werden, ein Minimum an Armaturen sowie funktionale Möbel wie Einbauwaschbecken über leichten Konstruktionen auf Metallfüßen, kleine Eckmöbel oder Einbauschränke zu wählen. Bei eingeschränktem Platz verzichtet man besser auf ein Bidet und installiert lediglich ein WC; die Badewanne wird durch eine Duschwanne ersetzt und das traditionelle Stand-WC durch ein eingelassenes oder Wandmodell. Unter der Ablage kann stets ein Möbelstück platziert werden, falls man zusätzlichen Lagerraum benötigt. Leichte Materialien wie Glas und Metall eignen sich hervorragend für kleine Räume.

es de bains
espaces
ts   Bathrooms
mall Places

ZIMMER IN
EN RÄUMEN

en espacios
equeños

On peut réaliser une salle de bains très jolie même si on ne dispose que de quelques mètres carrés. Aujourd'hui il existe des solutions très bien pensées avec des ressources très intelligentes qui exploitent aux maximum l'espace dont on dispose et permettent, à l'aide de quelques petits trucs, d'agrandir la pièce visuellement. Une petite salle de bains requière une simplicité des lignes ainsi qu'un minimum de meubles permettant de ranger le nécessaire. Dans ce type de salles de bains, l'aspect fonctionnel est très important ; le plus important étant de pouvoir placer tous les éléments utiles dans un espace réduit. La première règle consiste à leur ajouter de la luminosité : de ce fait on peut ouvrir une grande fenêtre sur l'extérieur ou employer des bloques de verre permettant de capter la lumière d'autres pièces. N'étant pas toujours possible d'user de ces recours une autre solution est de placer un grand miroir au-dessus du lavabo ou de plus petits à des points stratégiques. Les miroirs reflètent la lumière et font de cette façon paraître un espace optiquement plus grand (il ne faut toutefois pas en abuser). On doit aussi tenir compte de la couleur utilisée pour le sol et les parois. Les couleurs claires donnent une apparence plus grande à une pièce: les blancs, les tons crus et même les jaunes (très lumineux) sont très pertinents pour de petites pièces tandis que les couleurs plus foncées, bien que leur ajoutant beaucoup de personnalité, les privent de luminosité. Pour les revêtements, il est mieux d'utiliser des pièces de petite taille et de couleur claire. Si pourtant on désir installer, par exemple un bois foncé il est mieux de le combiner avec des éléments claires et lumineux. Dans les petites salles de bains on installe des sanitaires suspendus à la parois, un minimum de robinets, des meubles fonctionnels tels que lavabos entourés de structures légères et sur pieds métalliques, des petits meubles de coin ou des armoires encastrées. Dans un espace restreint il vaut mieux renoncer à un bidet et installer seulement des toilettes, substituer une douche à la baignoire et échanger un lavabo sur pied contre un lavabo suspendu ou encastré. Ainsi, si on a besoin d'un espace de rangement, on peut toujours placer un meuble en dessous. Les matériaux légers comme le verre et le métal sont très adéquats pour les espaces réduits.

Bathrooms in Small Places

Badezimmer in kleinen Räumen

SALLES DE BAINS POUR ESPACES REDUITS

Baños en espacios pequeños

Puede conseguirse un baño bello y muy práctico aunque no se disponga de muchos metros. En la actualidad, existen espacios muy pensados con recursos muy inteligentes que aprovechan al máximo el espacio, y a la vez, aplican algunos pequeños trucos que pueden ampliar visualmente una estancia. Un baño con poco espacio requiere simplicidad de líneas, así como un mobiliario mínimo que permita almacenar todo lo necesario. En este tipo de baños es muy importante el aspecto funcional, puesto que lo esencial es colocar todos los elementos útiles en un espacio reducido. La primera regla consiste en dotarlos de luminosidad: algunos proyectos abren una gran ventana al exterior o colocan ladrillos de pavés para contagiarse de la luz de otras estancias. Pero no siempre pueden utilizarse estos recursos: jugar con un gran espejo sobre el lavamanos o pequeñas lunas más reducidas pueden ser otra buena solución, puesto que los espejos multiplican la luz y pueden llegar a ampliar visualmente un espacio (siempre que no se abuse de ellos). El color utilizado en las paredes y los suelos también es un aspecto que tener en cuenta. Los colores claros parecen hacer más grande una habitación: los blancos, crudos e incluso amarillos (muy luminosos) son muy idóneos para habitaciones de pocos metros, mientras que los colores más oscuros, aunque añaden mucha personalidad, privan de luz. Para los revestimientos, es mejor utilizar piezas de pequeño tamaño de tonos muy claros. Si aun así se desea instalar, por ejemplo, madera oscura en el baño, es mejor combinarla con elementos claros y luminosos. En baños pequeños se utilizan sanitarios suspendidos en la pared, griferías mínimas o muebles funcionales como lavamanos encastrados sobre ligeras estructuras con patas metálicas, pequeños muebles rinconeros o armarios empotrados. En espacios reducidos es mejor renunciar al bidé y colocar sólo el sanitario, sustituir la bañera por un plato de ducha y cambiar el tradicional lavabo de pedestal por un modelo de pared o para encastrar. Así, si se necesita espacio para almacenar, siempre puede incorporarse un mueble bajo la encimera. Los materiales ligeros, como el cristal y el metal, son muy adecuados en espacios reducidos.

Salles de bains
pour espaces
Badezimmer in réduits
kleinen Räumen

BAÑOS EN
ESPACIOS
PEQUEÑOS

Bathrooms in
Small Places

Petit classique
Kleines klassisches
SMALL CLASSIC
Pequeño clásico

Répartition originale
Originelle Aufteilung
ORIGINAL DISTRIBUTION
Architects: **Navarro/Zalaja**
Distribución original

Photo © Jordi Miralles

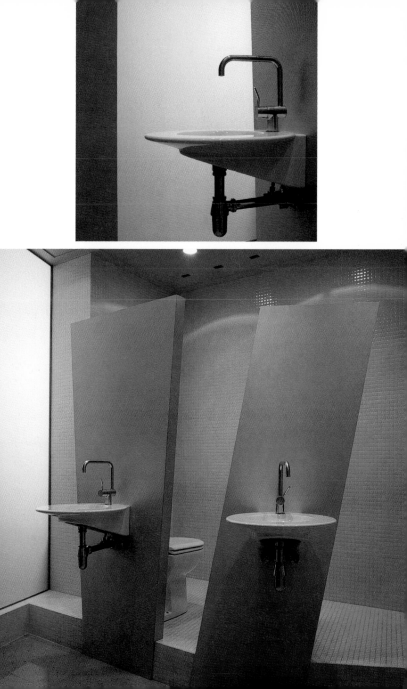

Tout bois
Nur Holz
ONLY WOOD
Sólo madera

Pour le bébé
Für Babies
FOR BABIES
Para niños

Transparent
Transparent
TRANSPARENT
Transparente

Architects: **Rataplan**

Style campagnard
Ländlicher Stil
COUNTRY STYLE
Estilo rural

Salles de bains de couleur
Farbige Badezimmer
COLORED BATHROOMS
Baños coloridos

The most daring interior designs opt for the use of only one color in the bathroom for the walls, furniture and coverings. Notwithstanding, some also combine it with more than one color, which endows it with a very modernday effect. Wise color use can visually alter the room whereby spaces may appear larger or smaller, or even, it may effect our mood. The rule of thumb is that light colors make the space seem larger, and dark colors do just the opposite, which is to make it seem smaller. Soft hues inspire and relax whereas, striking colors capture our attention, and can achieve a more elegant atmosphere with more personality. Normally, the conception of the bathroom is that of a space which invites us to relax. Consequently, what is traditionally chosen are soft colors and pastel tones of blue or light green, or neutral tones, which are associated with sea water and sand. Nevertheless, there is no set rule and the latest bathrooms, especially those installed in new homes with open spaces without walls, are opting for bright tones, like red, or for daring multicolor combinations. These designs grant vitality and originality to any space. They are particularly cherished in children's baths, since the children can wash and smarten up, in an ambience full of creativity. Other bathrooms opt for more formal colors such as black or gray tones which, above all, recreate an atmosphere of distinction. Yellow tones are ideal for achieving luminosity in the space, as too are the complete range of whites and light natural tones (ivory, cream, ...). In other baths the choice is to combine two or more colors within the same range, or, contrarily, to use two clearly differentiated tones, though perfectly capable of being combined, to attain contrasts. Bathrooms with light colors, dark colors or pastels ... what matters most is that the colors or the tones chosen, are well adapted to the personality and tastes, of the people who will use the bathroom.

Salles de bains de couleur
Farbige Badezimmer
COLORED
BATHROOMS
Baños coloridos

Die gewagtesten Kreationen setzen auf eine einzige Farbe im Badezimmer: für Wände, Möbel und Verkleidungen, wenngleich in einigen Räumen auch mehr als eine Farbe verwendet wird, wodurch ein sehr zeitgenössischer Eindruck erzielt wird. Ein intelligenter Einsatz von Farben kann ein Zimmer optisch verändern und Räume schaffen, die größer oder kleiner erscheinen, oder er kann unsere Stimmungslage beeinflussen. In der Regel werden Räume durch helle Farben optisch vergrößert und durch dunkle Farben scheinbar verkleinert; weiche Töne wirken inspirierend und entspannend, während kräftigere Farben unsere Aufmerksamkeit auf sich ziehen und einem Raum Eleganz und Persönlichkeit verleihen können. Normalerweise wird der Raum für ein Bad so konzipiert, dass er zur Entspannung einlädt, weshalb die klassischeren Ansätze von weichen Farben und Pastelltönen getragen werden, wobei man einem hellen Blau oder Grün und neutralen Farbtönen den Vorzug gibt, die mit dem Wasser des Meeres und Sand assoziiert werden. Da es jedoch keine festgeschriebenen Regeln gibt, setzt man bei neuen Bädern – vor allem bei jenen, die in neuen Wohnungen mit offenen, wandlosen Räumen eingerichtet werden – auf kräftige Farben wie Rot oder auf gewagte Farbkombinationen. Dank solcher Ideen wird jeder Raum mit Leben und Originalität erfüllt. Sie sind eine besonders glückliche Lösung in Kinderbadezimmern, weil die Kinder sich so in einer Umgebung voller Kreativität waschen und baden können. In anderen Bädern entschied man sich für gediegenere Farben wie Schwarz oder Grautöne, wodurch eine vor allem noble Atmosphäre geschaffen wird. Gelbtöne sind ideal, um Räumen viel Helligkeit zu geben, ebenso wie die gesamte Palette der Weiß- und Cremetöne in all ihren Schattierungen (Beige, Elfenbein, ...). In wiederum anderen Badezimmern finden sich Kombinationen von zwei oder mehr Tönen derselben Farbskala oder aber zwei vollkommen unterschiedliche Farbtöne, die allerdings hervorragend miteinander kombiniert werden können, um einen Kontrasteffekt zu erzielen. Ob nun Bäder in hellen, dunklen oder Pastellfarben – das Wichtigste ist, dass die ausgewählte Farbe oder die Farbtöne zum Geschmack und zur Persönlichkeit ihrer künftigen Benutzer passen.

Salles de bains de couleur
Colored Bathrooms
FARBIGE BADEZIMMER
Baños coloridos

Les créations audacieuses misent sur l'utilisation d'une seule couleur dans la salle de bains : les parois, le mobilier et les revêtements, tandis que d'autres préfèrent combiner plusieurs couleurs permettant d'obtenir un effet très moderne. Une sage utilisation des couleurs peut influencer optiquement une pièce, peut la faire paraître plus grande ou plus petite et peut également influencer notre état d'âme. En général, les couleurs claires créent un espace plus grand, tandis que les couleurs foncées l'amenuisent. Les tons doux inspirent et relaxent tandis que les couleurs plus fortes retiennent notre attention, et peuvent créent une ambiance élégante et ayant beaucoup de personnalité. Normalement, la salle de bains et conçue comme un endroit invitant à la relaxation et les options les plus classiques sont basées sur des couleurs douces et des tons pastels, utilisant du bleu et du vert clair ou des tons neutres rappelant l'eau de mer et le sable. Pourtant comme il n'existe pas de règles fixes, les salles de bains modernes, particulièrement celles qui sont dans les nouvelles constructions qui ont de grands espaces ouvert et sans parois, misent sur des tons forts, comme le rouge ou des combinaisons osées et multicolores. Elles désirent remplir chaque espace de vie et d'originalité. Ces options sont très appréciées dans les salles de bains pour enfants où ils peuvent se laver et se baigner dans un cadre plein de créativité. D'autres salles de bains optent pour des couleurs plus formelles comme le noir et les tons gris, qui recréent une ambiance distinguée. Les tons jaunes sont idéals pour donner beaucoup de luminosité de même que toutes la gamme des couleurs blanches et écrues dans toutes leur variété (crème, ivoire …). Dans certaines salles de bains on combine deux ou plusieurs couleurs de la même gamme chromatique, ou on utilise des tons complètement différents pouvant être bien combinés entre eux, afin d'obtenir un contraste. Des salles de bains claires, foncées ou pastels … le plus important est que les couleurs et les tons choisis s'adaptent à la personnalité et aux goûts de ceux qui vont les utiliser.

Colored
Bathrooms
Farbige Badezimmer
SALLES DE BAINS
DE COULEUR
Baños coloridos

Las creaciones más atrevidas apuestan por utilizar un solo color en el cuarto de baño: en paredes, muebles y revestimientos, aunque en algunos espacios se combina más de un color, lo que consigue un efecto muy actual. Un sabio empleo de los colores puede llegar a alterar visualmente una estancia, al crear espacios que pueden parecer más grandes o más pequeños, o bien afectar a nuestro estado de ánimo. Por norma general, los colores claros generan un espacio más amplio y los más oscuros parecen empequeñecerlo; los tonos suaves inspiran y relajan, mientras que los colores más fuertes atraen nuestra atención y pueden conseguir un ambiente elegante y con personalidad. Normalmente, el baño se concibe con un espacio que invita a la relajación, por lo que las opciones más clásicas apuestan por colores suaves y tonos pastel, utilizando el azul y el verde claro o los tonos neutros, relacionados con el agua del mar y la arena. Pero como no existe regla fija, los nuevos baños, especialmente los que se incorporan en las nuevas viviendas con espacios abiertos y sin paredes, apuestan por tonos fuertes como el rojo, o por combinaciones atrevidas multicolor. Son apuestas que llenan de vida y originalidad cualquier espacio. Estas opciones son muy agradecidas en baños infantiles, puesto que los niños pueden asearse y bañarse en un entorno repleto de creatividad. Otros baños apuestan por colores más formales como el negro o los tonos grises, colores que recrean especialmente un ambiente distinguido. Los tonos amarillos son ideales para conseguir espacios muy luminosos, al igual que toda la gama de colores blancos y crudos en todas sus variantes (color crema, marfil…). Otros baños optan por combinar dos o más colores de una misma gama cromática, o bien utilizar dos tonos claramente diferenciados, aunque muy combinables entre sí, para conseguir un efecto de contraste. Baños de colores claros, oscuros o pastel… lo más importante es que el color o los tonos elegidos se adapten a la personalidad y el gusto de aquellos que vayan a utilizarlo.

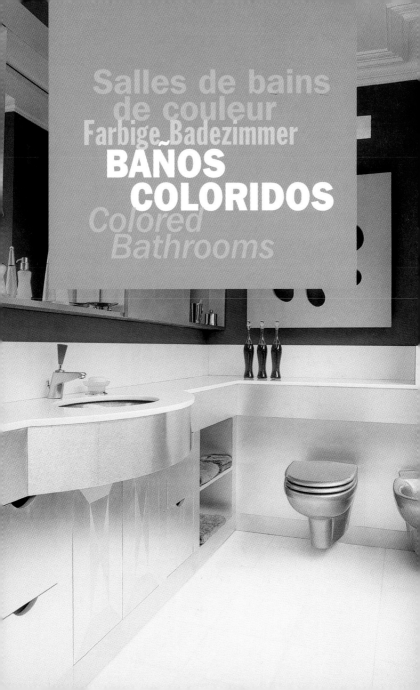

Salles de bains
de couleur
Farbige Badezimmer
BAÑOS
COLORIDOS
*Colored
Bathrooms*

L'art de la Mosaïque
Mosaik-Kunst
MOSAIC ART
Arte mosaico

BLUE BATHROOM

Photo © José Luis Hausmann

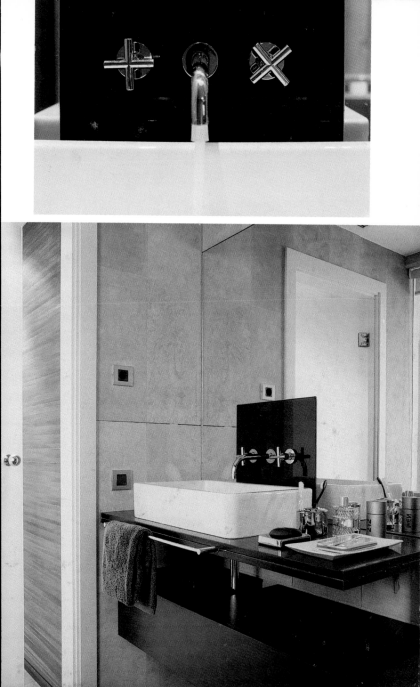

Bicolore
Zweifarbig
BICOLOR
Bicolor

Interiorists: **Pipe Dreams**

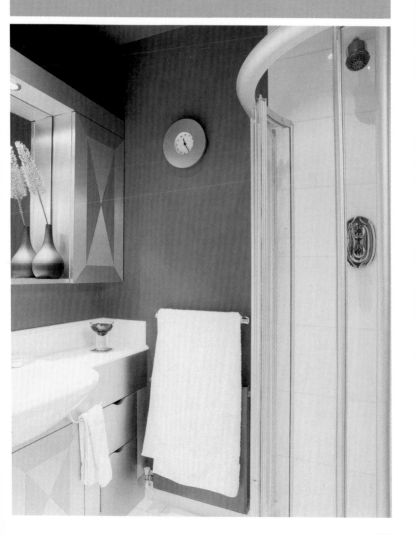

Salle de bains rose
Rosa Badezimmer
PINK BATHROOM
Baño rosa

L'art violet
Lila Kunst
VIOLET ART
Arte lila

Interiorists: **Pipe Dreams**

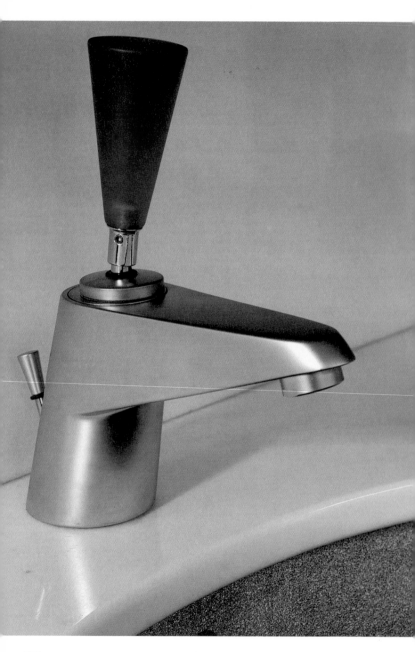

RED ISLAND

Île rouge
Rote Insel
Isla roja

Architect: **Holger Kleine**

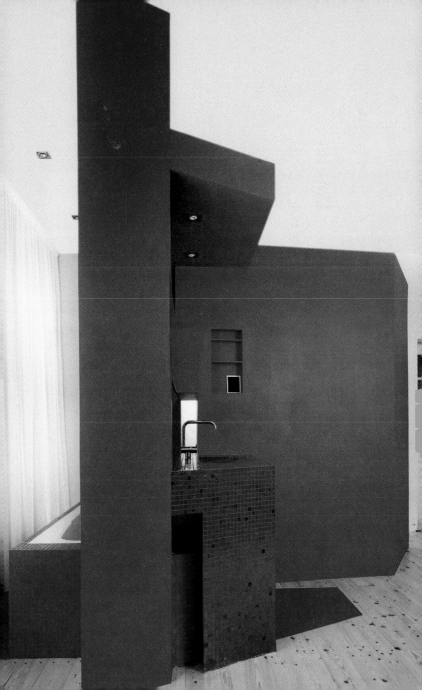

An abstract bathroom inside the "three voice interior" Apartment (Babelsberger Straße, Berlin) by the architect Holger Kleine.

Innerhalb der „Dreistimmigen Wohnung" (Babelsberger Straße, Berlin) des Architekten Holger Kleine, ein Badezimmerprojekt, das durch seine Abstraktheit wirkt.

A l'intérieur de l'appartement « intérieur à trois voix » (Babelsberger Straße, Berlin) de l'architecte Holger Kleine, une salle de bains abstraite faisant de l'effet.

Un baño abstracto en el apartamento "interior tres voces" (Babelsberger Straße, Berlín) del arquitecto Holger Kleine.

Vert sur fond bleu
Grün auf Blau
Architect: **Holger Kleine**
GREEN ON BLUE
Verde sobre azul

Explosion de couleurs
Explosion der Farben
COLOR EXPLOSION
Explosión de color

Photo © Jordi Miralles

Tradition recuperé
Anlehnung an die Tradition
RECUPERATED TRADITION
Tradición recuperada

Photo © Lluís Miras

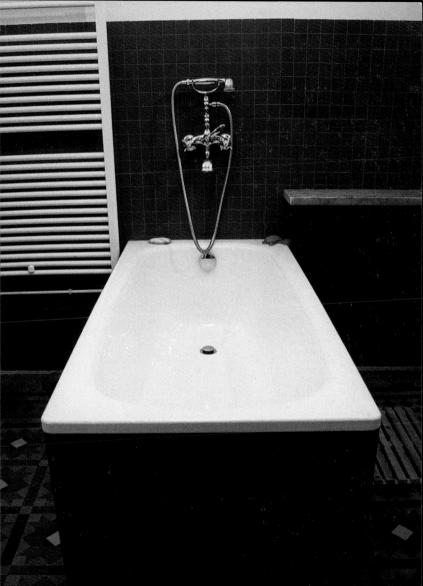

Salles de bains claires
Helle Badezimmer
BRIGHT
BATHROOMS
Baños claros

Some bathrooms are conceived to be opened out to the light and to take in the exterior surroundings. Some can easily achieve this because, thanks to a privileged distribution, a large window can be opened to the exterior and the bathtub placed in front of it, or each of the zones within, can be designed so as to be privileged with abundant natural light. With other bathrooms, though, we must make use of other resources so that they appear to have more light. A few of the tricks that can be put to use are, the use of light-colored and visually light materials, and the choice of under-sized bathroom fittings. Consequently, a space of limited size or set in an unprivileged place, can be transformed into a bright bathroom. Light-colored floors are important for reflecting light. Light shades of any material, stoneware, marble, wood or synthetic materials, should be chosen, which will augment lightness. A good option are light-colored beechwood, pine or oak parkets (treated to resist water and humidity), as they grant warmth to the bathroom as well. Another trick is to cover the floor and the walls with the same light-colored, bright material. Open spaces without walls like lofts, adopt other tricks to obtain natural light from other zones such as, placing transparent elements as dividers. Similarly, bathrooms conceived as single spaces, can denote different zones by the use of small white or glass walls. Sliding glass doors, glass partitions, or half-height walls, all favor the obtainment of a more luminous effect. If the distribution is designed in such a way that it does not obstruct the circulation of the light, a more luminous bathroom will be the result. It is key not to overload the shelves and the high pieces of furniture. The most voluminous furniture should be up against the wall, thus leaving the central area uncluttered. Lighting is also of utmost importance. Artificial light alters the color of walls, furniture and the complements. Each zone must be properly illuminated and if possible, halogen bulbs should be used, as they afford a more brilliant and clearer light.

Salles de bains claires

Helle Badezimmer

BRIGHT BATHROOMS

Baños claros

Schon die Konzeption mancher Badezimmer bringt die Absicht zum Ausdruck, sie dem Licht zu öffnen und die äußere Umgebung in sie einzubeziehen. In einigen Räumen wird dies problemlos erreicht, da aufgrund ihrer günstigen Raumaufteilung ein großes Fenster eingebaut und die Badewanne diesem gegenüber platziert werden kann, oder ein jeder Bereich so angelegt ist, dass er von Tageslicht durchflutet wird. Andere Bäder jedoch erfordern besondere Tricks, um heller zu erscheinen. Der Einsatz heller und optisch leichter wirkender Materialien oder die Wahl von kleineren Möbeln und WCs sind einige Optionen, die einen Raum von wenigen Quadratmetern oder in ungünstiger Lage in ein lichterfülltes Bad verwandeln können. Auch Böden in hellen Farben sind wichtige Lichtreflektoren. Bei jedem Material (Steinzeug, Glaskeramik, Marmor, Holz oder Kunststoffe ...) müssen helle Töne gewählt werden, um das Licht zu unterstützen. Helles Parkett, z. B. aus Buche, Kiefer oder Eiche (mit Behandlung zum Schutz gegen Wasser und Feuchtigkeit), ist eine gute Wahl, das dem Bad eine warme Atmosphäre gibt. Ein weiterer Kunstgriff besteht im Auskleiden des Bodens und der Wände mit ein und demselben hellen und glänzenden Material. Bei offenen und wandlosen Räumen (Loftstil) kommen einige Tricks zur Anwendung, um von dem in anderen Bereichen einfallenden Tageslicht zu profitieren, so z. B. durch den Einsatz von durchsichtigen Trennelementen wie bei den als Einheit konzipierten Bädern, in denen die jeweiligen Bereiche durch halbhohe weiße oder gläserne Mauern definiert werden. Glasschiebetüren, verglaste Trennwände oder halbhohe Mauern tragen dazu bei, einen Raum mehr Helligkeit ausstrahlen zu lassen. Ebenso kann ein Bad lichter gestaltet werden, indem es so angelegt wird, dass der Einfall des Lichtes nicht behindert wird. Das wichtigste ist hierbei, Fensterbretter und hohe Möbel nicht zu sehr zu überladen und kompaktere Möbelstücke an den Wänden aufzustellen, damit der zentrale Bereich nicht verstellt wird. Ein weiterer entscheidender Faktor ist die Beleuchtung, denn künstliches Licht verändert die Farbe von Wänden, Möbeln und Ausstattungselementen. Jeder einzelne Bereich muss korrekt beleuchtet sein, wobei nach Möglichkeit Halogenlampen zu verwenden sind, da sie ein helleres und reineres Licht spenden.

Salles de bains
claires
Bright Bathrooms
**HELLE
BADEZIMMER**
Baños claros

I y a des salles de bains qui naissent avec l'intention de s'ouvrir à la lumière et de se remplir du paysage extérieur. Certains espaces peuvent le réaliser sans problèmes, jouissant d'un emplacement privilégié, pouvant leur permettre d'ouvrir une très grande vitre et d'y mettre la baignoire devant, ou d'inonder chacune des zones d'une lumière abondante. D'autres salles de bains doivent cependant avoir recours à d'autre solutions pour paraître plus lumineuses : Utiliser des matériaux clairs et d'apparence légère ou choisir un mobilier et des sanitaires de petite taille sont quelques-uns des trucs permettant de rendre plus lumineux une pièce de petite dimension ou mal située. Les sols clairs sont également de bons réflecteurs de lumière. Pour augmenter la clarté, il est bon que tous les matériaux choisis soient de tons clairs (de grès, mosaïque, marbre, bois ou matériaux synthétiques …). Les parquets clairs de hêtre, de pin ou de chêne (traités préalablement pour supporter l'eau et l'humidité), sont aussi une bonne option et donnent une certaine qualité à la pièce. Un autre truc consiste à recouvrir le sol et les parois d'un même matériel claire et brillant. Les espaces ouverts et sans parois (du type loft) emploient certains trucs pour capter la lumière naturelle d'autres zones, comme des séparations en éléments transparents. De même que les salles de bains conçues comme une pièce unique, on peut déterminer les différentes zones à l'aide de petits murets blancs ou de verre. Les portes coulissantes et les cloisons de verre ou les murets à mi-hauteur permettent aussi d'obtenir un effet plus lumineux. On peut augmenter la clarté en répartissant les éléments de façon à permettre à la lumière de circuler : la clé en est de ne pas surcharger les étagères et les meubles hauts et d'appuyer les meubles volumineux à la parois pour dégager le centre. L'éclairage est aussi un facteur important, la lumière artificielle altérant la couleur des parois, des meubles et des accessoires. On doit éclairer correctement chacune des zones et si possible, utiliser des lampes halogènes qui sont plus claires et brillantes.

Bright Bathrooms
Helle Badezimmer
SALLES DE BAINS CLAIRES
Baños claros

Hay cuartos de baño que nacen con la intención de abrirse a la luz, de contagiarse del paisaje exterior. Algunos espacios lo consiguen sin problemas, puesto que, por su privilegiada distribución, pueden permitirse abrir un gran ventanal y colocar la bañera enfrente, o proyectar cada una de sus zonas de forma que se inunden de abundante luz natural. Otros baños, sin embargo, precisan recursos extra para que parezcan más luminosos: utilizar materiales claros y visualmente muy ligeros, o elegir el mobiliario y los sanitarios de tamaño reducido son algunos de los trucos que pueden transformar en un baño luminoso un espacio de reducidos metros o de difícil ubicación. Los suelos de colores claros son también importantes reflectores de luz. Deben elegirse tonos claros de cualquier material (gres, gresite, mármol, madera o materiales sintéticos…) para potenciar la claridad. Los parqués claros como el haya, el pino y el roble (tratados para que soporten el agua y la humedad) son una buena opción porque añaden, además, calidez al baño. Otro truco consiste en cubrir el suelo y las paredes con un mismo material claro y brillante. Los espacios abiertos y sin paredes (tipo loft) utilizan algunos trucos para recibir la luz natural de otras zonas, como colocar elementos transparentes a modo de separaciones, al igual que los baños concebidos como una única estancia, que pueden zonificar cada una de las partes con muretes blancos o de cristal. Las puertas correderas de cristal, los tabiques acristalados o los muretes a media altura ayudan a obtener un efecto más luminoso. Puede conseguirse un baño más claro distribuyéndolo de forma que no entorpezca la circulación de la luz: la clave está en no sobrecargar excesivamente las repisas y los muebles altos y apoyar en las paredes el mobiliario más voluminoso para que quede más despejada la zona central. La iluminación es también un factor clave, puesto que la luz artificial altera el color de las paredes, los muebles y los complementos. Debe iluminarse correctamente cada una de las zonas y, a ser posible, utilizar bombillas halógenas, puesto que son más claras y brillantes.

Salles de bains claires
~Helle Badezimmer
BAÑOS CLAROS
Bright Bathrooms

URBAN SPACE

Espace urbain
Urbaner Raum

Espacio urbano

Jour et nuit
Tag und Nacht
DAY AND NIGHT
Día y noche

Photo © José Luis Hausmann

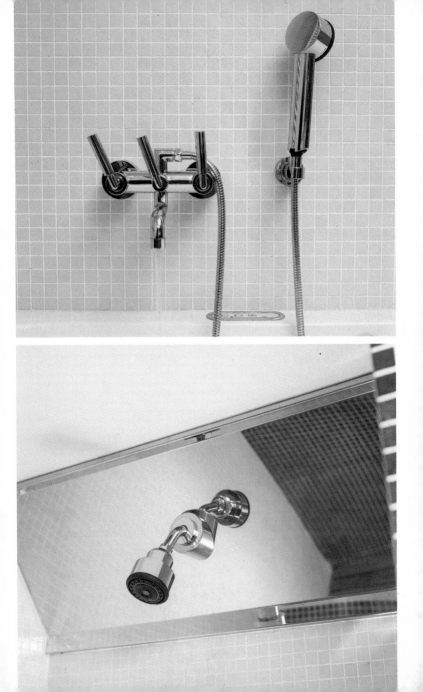

WHITE BATHROOM

Bain blanc
Weißes Badezimmer

Baño blanco

Architects: **Vincent Van Duysen Architects**

Photo © Eugeni Pons

Boîte de cristal
Kristallbox
CRISTAL BOX
Caja de cristal

Matériaux naturels
Natürliche Materialien
NATURAL MATERIALS
Materiales naturales

Architect: **Alberto Kalach**

Photo © Undine Pröhl

DIRECTORY

firms

Photo credits:

Carlos Domínguez: *p.54, p.145, p.333*

Chis Gascoigne (VIEW Pictures): *p.107, p.249*

Christopher Wesnofske: *p.12*

Erhard Pfeiffer: *p.100*

Eugeni Pons: *p.11, p.67, p.81, p.89*

Hedrich Blessing: *p.69*

Hervè Abbadie: *p.12*

Ignacio Martínez: *p.46*

Interstampa: *p.52, p.53, p.54*

Jeff Heatley: *p.89*

Jordi Miralles: *p.50, p.24, p.25, p.97, p.126, p.128, p.129, p.131, p.331*

Jörg Hempel: *p.104*

José Luis Hausmann: *p.17, p.55, p.67, p.73, p.129*

Lluís Miras: *p.193*

Matteo Piazza: *p.50, p.64*

Miquel Tres: *p.49*

Mihail Moldoveanu: *p.38*

Montse Garriga: *p.8, p.20, p.24, p.30, p.45, p.55*

Nick Hufton (VIEW Pictures): *p.75*

Patrick Reynolds: *p.93*

Pere Planells: *p.9, p.19, p.22, p.26, p.27, p.28, p.29, p.51, p.73*

Phillippe Saharoff: *p.93*

Reiner Lautwein: *p.112*

Ricardo Labougle: *p.10, p.13, p.79*

Richard Glover: *p.40*

Ross Honeysett: *p.11, p.59*

Thomas Riehle: *p.103*

Undine Pröhl: *p.35, p.101*

Special thanks to **Eduardo de la Peña** *and* **Justo García Navarro,** *professors of Universidad Politécnica de Madrid (ETSI Agrónomos - Departamento de Construcción y Vías Rurales)*